Are Ye Not Gods?

True inner messages and teachings of Jesus explained

By Eileen McCourt

Are Ye Not Gods?

True inner messages and teachings of Jesus explained

By Eileen McCourt

Are Ye Not Gods? - True inner messages and teachings of Jesus explained. This book was first published in Great Britain in paperback during March 2017.

ISBN-13: 978-1544026503

CONTENTS

ABOUT THE AUTHOR

Eileen McCourt is a retired school teacher of English and History with a Master's degree in History from University College Dublin.

She is also a Reiki Grand Master teacher and practitioner, having qualified in Ireland, England and Spain, and has introduced many of the newer modalities of Reiki healing energy into Ireland for the first time, from Spain and England.

Eileen holds regular workshops and healing sessions in Elysium Wellness, Newry, County Down and in Angel Times, Limerick.

This is Eileen's ninth book.

Previous publications include:

- '***Living the Magic***', published in December 2014
- '***This Great Awakening***', September 2015
- '***Spirit Calling! Are You Listening?***', January 2016
- '***Working With Spirit: A World of Healing***', January 2016
- '***Life's But A Game! Go With The Flow!***', March 2016
- '***Rainbows, Angels and Unicorns!***', April 2016
- '***........And That's The Gospel Truth!***', September 2016
- '***The Almost Immaculate Deception! The Greatest Scam in History?***', September 2016

All publications are available from Amazon online and are in Angel and Holistic centres around the country, as specified on the website.

Eileen is currently working on her tenth book, '***Jesus: Lost and Found!'***, of which this book, '***Are ye not Gods?'*** is an off-shoot.

Website: www.celestialhealing8.co.uk

Note to the reader

It is generally accepted by both scholars and reading public alike that the four canonical gospels, Mark, Matthew, Luke and John cannot be considered as reliable historical documents. They were written 40 to 70 years after the death of Jesus, and were never intended to be historical documents. They are permeated with historical inaccuracies, contradictions, bias, copying and sloppy re-editing.

Having said that, they do, however, have value as theological documents. The information contained in them was handed down orally for over 40 years. The writings were intended to glorify Jesus in competition with other Roman gods of the time. And when we take all this into consideration and allow for the bias, there is still valuable information about Jesus' teachings to be found in the residue.

Most of the information I have quoted is taken from these canonical gospels. Why? Because they were the specific gospels selectively hand-picked by the early fathers of the newly fledged Christian Church, at the Council of Nicea in 325 C.E. to be the basis for the new religion of the Roman Empire, that new religion which would come to dominate the world. And they are the specific gospels that we have been taught down through the centuries as containing the teachings of Jesus.

However, those teachings have been misrepresented, distorted and manipulated by those who have sought to control us for their own devious purposes.

This book is an attempt to explain True inner teachings of Jesus, the true inner teachings of Jesus that have been kept from us for so long, and not just the external teachings which have been presented to us and interpreted for us by those with their own personal agenda.

For the purposes of this book, I have used the *Sunrise Good News Bible* published by Collins.

There are of course, other sources besides the New Testament for the teachings of Jesus. A lot were found at Nag Hammadi in Egypt in the middle of the 20th century, all copies of the originals, which were deliberately and systematically burnt by the Christian Church in the early centuries, in an effort to stamp out what they termed heresy and to establish itself as the all-powerful, the sole religious authority on earth, commanding total and complete obedience and submission to its dogmas and teachings.

I have not used these more recent sources for this book. And why not? Simply because this book is an attempt to rectify the misrepresentations in the four canonical gospels. That's all!

The sources found at Nag Hammadi and elsewhere are reserved for my next book, ***'Jesus Lost and Found'.*** That was intended as my ninth book. However, this present book has materialised somewhere along the way as an off-shoot from that, which I did not foresee when I began to write it! More proof indeed, if I ever needed any, that these books are definitely not being written by me. They only bear my name in order to manifest them in this physical world. I am only the channel, the conduit. Greater forces by far than me are at work here, and all I can do is go with the flow. And how happy I am to do that! How privileged and honoured I feel! And at the same time, how humbled!

Who knows what other sources are hidden within the Vatican walls? Is it not strange that we have never been told about the missing years of Jesus? About those missing years from he was twelve years of age until he began his ministry at the age of thirty? Or about his connection with Mary Magdalene, to whom he himself referred as "*The woman who knows all*"? Or that we have no actual writings of Jesus himself? Perhaps they too lie beneath the desert of Egypt or somewhere in Persia, or in the caves in India, awaiting discovery. But we can be sure that when the time is right, whatever we need to know will be revealed to us, not by any church administration, but by the synchronistic events that constantly manifest in our inter-connected worlds, our inter-connected universes and throughout our entire cosmos.

Everything in its own time!

Namaste!

Eileen McCourt

16th March 2017

ACKNOWLEDGEMENTS

I wish to thank my publishers, Don Hale OBE and Dr. Steve Green for their tireless work, their advice and their patience.

My sincere thanks once again to my family and to my wonderful friends who are always supporting me in my Spiritual work. You all know who you are!

Thanks to all of you who are buying my books and cds and for your kind and generous comments.

Thank you to all who come to my workshops and courses and share all that beautiful energy and all those amazing experiences.

To all those who have written reviews, both in my books and on Amazon, a special word of thanks. You are greatly appreciated!

And as always, I give thanks for all the wonderful blessings that constantly pour down on all of us in this amazing Universe. We are greatly loved and always looked after!

Eileen McCourt

16th March 2017

Are Ye Not Gods?

FOREWORD

We here on planet earth are merely a microcosmic element of the macrocosm that is entire creation. We are very small fish in an overwhelmingly vast pond. We are tiny pawns in a game so powerful that we cannot even begin to imagine its entirety.

But nevertheless, we are still players in that game, still inherent components of the great plan, the grand design. There is a plan for humanity, but we are not the architect. We are not at the controls. We are not at the helm. We are not steering the ship. And we cannot see the entire plan. We are severely limited by our earthly vision. All for a reason.

The dawning of the age of Aquarius!

This is it!

Something big is happening! Something real big! Something beyond man's full comprehension. In the words of the Phil Collins' song: '*I can feel it coming in the air .... I've been waiting for this moment all my life.*'

The New Age! The Age of Enlightenment! The Age of Knowing!

Mankind is ready, mankind is on the cusp, on the verge of a massive shift in consciousness, a massive transformation in spiritual awareness, an irreversible transformation, so profound, that the doors into the realm of Spirit are opening as never before in the entire history of humanity.

We can all feel a grand new tomorrow coming on! A beautiful new dawning! A new world!

Our planet earth is in transition. Our planet earth is in ascension. Ascending from the dense third dimension frequency to the higher, lighter fourth and fifth level frequencies.

How blessed we are to be living in these wondrous times, the most exciting of times, yet also the most unpredictable of times!

We live in a world and in a universe amongst countless other worlds and universes. But more significantly, we live on a particular energy vibrational level, amongst a plethora of other vibrational energy frequencies throughout the whole of creation. There are worlds beyond worlds, civilizations beyond civilizations. These are the worlds of energy, not worlds of dense matter or form such as our planet earth. We are multi-dimensional, inter-dimensional, inter-planetary travellers, all inter-dependent and inter-connected in the vastness of the Great Universal Energy, the God Energy, outside of which absolutely nothing or no-one can exist. The veil between our earthly world of matter and these other levels of energy vibrational frequencies is now very thin, made thinner by the planetary alignment of 2012.

We are all destined to transcend physicality, and see beyond the limiting boundaries of our earthly human body, which, after all, is merely a physical vehicle to transport our immortal soul through this life-time.

Every so often, a highly evolved soul, one who has preceded us on the journey, one who has already transcended physicality, one who has already transcended death and the dense world of matter and form, one who has already attained Enlightenment, reaches out to us, returns to our dense earth vibration, offering us help and trying to show us the way. Such names as Buddha, Muhammed, and in our own times, Mahatma Gandhi, all spring to mind.

And yes! Jesus!

Most definitely the most famous person in history!

To understand the teachings of Jesus of first century Jewish Palestine, we have to transcend the physical, to go beyond earthly dimensions and enter the higher vibrational energy frequencies. We have to reach beyond the historian's boundaries, beyond the radar of the five limiting physical senses, into the spirit worlds, where time is non-existent, where the past and future merge into only the present, the here-and-now, stretching into infinity, unending, eternal, devoid of any linear, time or spatial demarcations.

We are not just physical bodies. We are Spiritual beings having a physical experience, embodied here on this earth plane, on this dense vibrational earth frequency, in order to raise our own Spiritual consciousness and the Spiritual consciousness of all humanity. The Spiritual evolution of our immortal soul is the sole (!) reason for our life on this planet earth at this point in time.

Eternity is not something which begins at our physical death and goes on from there into infinity. Eternity is, truly, here and now! Yes! We are living in eternity right here and now! This present earth journey is just one of our many such journeys on our long walk-about across eternity.

When we complete our freely chosen, self-appointed, individually designated plan for this time around on planet earth, we return to the world of Spirit, the worlds of higher vibrational energy frequencies, where we continue to evolve and gain further knowledge as we progress up the Spiritual ladder, up the cosmic elevator.

Spirit life, contrary to what is taught by orthodox religions, is one of constant progress through the various realms of the spirit universe. There is no lying around on a fluffy cloud singing hymns or playing a harp! Not at all! How boring what would be! And for all eternity! It is all about soul progress, soul learning, soul development, soul evolution.

The Spirit world is a multi-layered and extremely intricate web of non-physical realities. Much like an onion, its core is light, the layers becoming more and more dense from the inside out, until that core pure light becomes created form, becomes matter, becomes life. The spirits of those who have passed exist within these various, progressive layers of consciousness and light, and when we become spiritually aware of these layers, we become aware of the existence of those spirits within them. In this way, our loved ones connect with us spiritually, as do all in the lighter and higher realms, such as the Saints, Angels, Masters. The Spirit world is, literally, overflowing with help, and that help is all passed down through to the physical layer in which we live.

And so our evolution continues beyond this life, and the next, and the next! This is the way it is for each and every one of us! No exceptions!

And so it was and is for Jesus!

Jesus too, was progressing up the Spiritual ranks, up the cosmic elevator for a long, long time. He too had many life-times on this earth plane. He is now, and has been, for a very long earth time, in the highest evolutionary energy frequency vibrational level.

Now known as Sananda, a highly evolved Ascended Master, now in the highest ranks, he was, during one of his life-times here on earth, known as Yeshua, Jesus of Nazareth. Just like us, Yeshua was human, and just like us at present, on one of his many walk-abouts across eternity, but for Jesus, that was to be his last incarnation on earth.

Jesus came down the vibrational corridor just like all the rest of us mortals, for a life-time here on planet earth. But he came from a very high energy frequency level, far beyond what we can even imagine!

That was 2,000 earth years ago.

Sananda now. Yeshua then. Yeshua ben Joseph

Jesus was, among other things, a mystic, a spiritual teacher, a shaman and a prophet. And it is from the much higher spiritual energy vibrational frequency that Jesus continues to reach out to us here on this dense earth energy vibrational frequency, teaching us, guiding us, inviting us to follow him along the path that he himself has already trod and levelled out for us.

Mystics have walked amongst us in every age, those have been in contact with other worlds and other vibrations. Jesus was one such.

And how does mysticism differ from mainstream religion?

Mysticism shows that the key to our Spiritual awareness, the key to progressing up the Spiritual cosmic elevator is to raise our Spiritual consciousness. And how exactly do we manage that? We raise our Spiritual consciousness by realising and accepting that we have everything we need inside ourselves, as part of our own divinity, and hence with our own unlimited potentiality.

In contrast, what does mainstream religion teach?

Mainstream religion teaches that we must look outside ourselves, to external sources, if we are ever going to find salvation. And an external church will do all for us! An external church will make the rules and promise us eternal rewards if we obey those rules without questioning. An attractive, appealing package indeed! No responsibility, no thinking needed, just tag along with a pre-packaged deal! How convenient!

It must surely be one of the greatest ironies of history that

Christianity changed Jesus into a saviour who saved us, whereas, in reality, Jesus came to teach us how to save ourselves by finding the kingdom of God within ourselves, and not from external sources, not from external mechanisms, not from external promptings and not from leaning on external crutches.

Jesus came to us with a message. A message about how to live a better, more fulfilling life. A message about what life here on planet earth is all about. A message about who and what we are in the entire totality of creation. A message about how to change from the hatred and violence of the fear based approach to life to the unconditional love of the heart-centered approach to life. And that message was delivered by Jesus to suit different levels of Spiritual consciousness.

Simply because not everyone was ready!

"*He that hath ears to hear, let them hear.*" (Matthew 11:15)

Jesus was the master of metaphors, the master of psychology, one who had already transcended all the human stuff, delivering his teachings mostly in simple parables for everyone at the time listening to him to understand. Jesus sowed the seeds, but now, 2,000 years later, where our Spiritual consciousness is much higher than then, we can access the more advanced teachings, the inner meanings, the true message that Jesus delivered.

A liberating message! A message by which we could claim our rightful divinity!

And what did we do?

First, we crucified the messenger.

Then we discarded the message.

Then we deified and mythologised the messenger! Through the political process of turning Jesus into a god for the expediency of the needs of the Roman Empire!

Then we once again retrieved the message!

But! We then distorted that message. We then created a fear-instilling God, a male person somewhere up beyond the clouds, judging us, and if we failed to please him, condemning us to an eternity of everlasting punishment in fire in a place called hell.

We need to get the hell out of here!

We created a religion centered around the crucifixion of Jesus. A controlling, manipulative, coercive, absolutist, dictatorial, no-opposition-tolerated religion, built on the artificial, flimsy fabric of fear and guilt.

Where is Jesus and his love, tolerance and compassion for all people in this?

Jesus on the cross! The iconic image, before us everywhere, of what religion is supposed to be all about!

We see images of Buddha, a smiling, laughing, carefree Buddha, totally at peace with himself and with the world, fat belly full to bursting with all the food he gets! The joy of living! The joy of understanding! The joy of just being, the joy of being at one with the universal God energy!

But what do we see outside and inside every orthodox church?

Jesus suffering and dying on the cross! Nothing about his life, nothing about his teachings, nothing about the messages he came to give us! No joy! No happiness! No laughter! No exhilaration or joy in the magic and in the awe of just being!

We need to take Jesus down from that cross! We need to stop seeing the Crucifixion as the main event in Jesus' life! What about the joy of his teachings? What about the joy that is ours when we take those teachings on board?

And what about the images of Jesus' mother that we see inside and outside every orthodox church?

A beautiful face, but a suffering face, always turned downwards. Sad, sad, sad! No joy, no happiness, nothing that expresses anything other than pain and suffering!

Doom and gloom all around! How different from the Buddha and Eastern beliefs!

But Jesus is not all about doom and gloom! He brought teachings of joy, light, truth and abundance!

It is ironic, indeed, that never in the history of humanity, has any church, any religion, or any government based its ethos, moral code or beliefs on the teachings of Jesus! The teachings of Jesus have, sadly and regrettably, never yet been tried out! Fact!

"He that hath ears to hear, let them hear."

Jesus did not force his message or any of his teachings on us. He simply delivered the message to those who were ready to hear, to those whose Spiritual awareness, those whose Spiritual consciousness was sufficiently raised to enable them to accept what he was saying. But not just to those. Jesus delivered his message and teachings to everyone. That was why he delivered his teachings to two different levels. To those who were not on a high enough Spiritual energy frequency level, he spoke in parables, to make it all easier from them to understand.

This book aims to explain the true inner message, the true inner teachings of Jesus, the true inner teachings of Jesus which orthodox religion has indeed denied us. The true inner teachings which have been kept from us by those who saw a need to keep them from us, those whose main aim was to control us.

And when we understand the true, inner teachings, we can access the inner reality that we are all of divine nature, we are all designed to be co-creators with God, and we are all destined to transcend physicality and the worlds of matter and form.

And when we understand the true, inner teachings of Jesus, we will understand clearly why we are here on planet earth at this point in time, we will understand clearly that we have unlimited potential within ourselves, and we will understand clearly that we are all united in the Oneness of the great Universal Consciousness, the great Universal Energy of Totality, the great Universal Energy of Infinity that is God.

It is time for us to claim our true identity! We have always been told we are sinners, so far below Jesus that we will never get to where he is!

But that's not what Jesus told us!

"Are ye not gods, as I am?"

So! Are you ready?

Are you ready to hear the inner, true meanings of the teachings of Jesus?

"He that hath ears...."

REVIEWS

Instead of being just a passive follower of Christ, this book encourages the reader to raise their consciousness and ACT in a Christ-like manner.

Go on! Why not give it a try!

Clare Bowman, Spiritual Historian

Yet another beautiful and wonderful book by gifted author Eileen McCourt. As you read this book it will reach and touch your soul as the author gets to the truth of who we really are.

It's a must to read and it's my honour to call you my friend!

Francesca Brown
The Angel Whisperer

McCourt has again given us another vital instalment in her analysis of the roots of the Christian Church, its teachings and its raison d'être.

In 'Are Ye Not Gods?', McCourt, again, offers a view of the teachings of Christianity that is both forensic and revolutionary. Through these volumes, we are given a picture of manipulation and

control by a supposedly 'Spiritual organisation'. However, rather than 'throw the baby out with the bathwater', we are given a picture of the true message of Christianity, or the message that Jesus Christ meant to give us. We are all divine, we are all of 'Christ Consciousness'. It is our role to navigate our way past the man-made obstacles and again embrace our true, 'Spiritually enlightened' state, that is ultimately our real essence.

In 'Are Ye Not Gods?', we are given a refreshing view of the 'Spiritual Christ', whose simple message is, we are all one, certainly not what the Church would have us believe. A timely message, given the daily revelations of abuse perpetrated by this organisation. McCourt would argue that with the increased energies of this time in history, we must look to the 'real' Spiritual teachings of the Christ and leave behind the life-denying philosophy that we have been mired in for too long. A truly Spiritual and increasingly necessary message!

Declan Quigley, Shamanic Practitioner and co-founder of The Irish School of Shamanic Studies.

PART ONE: FIRST-CENTURY JEWISH PALESTINE

Chapter 1

Concept of God in first-century Jewish Palestine

The Entity, the life force now known to us as Jesus, reincarnated from the higher Spiritual realms as Yeshua, Yeshua ben Joseph, Yeshua son of Joseph, 2000 years ago in first-century Jewish Palestine.

A world very different from our 21st century world!

Today, we are on the upward spiral spiritually, as more and more of us begin to awaken, as more and more of us begin to raise our spiritual consciousness, as more and more of us begin to increase our spiritual awareness, as more and more of us begin to realise and accept that there is no separation between us and God, as more and more of us accept our divinity, our divine essence. We are all One in the infinity and totality of the Universal Consciousness of the God Energy.

How different from first century Jewish Palestine!

The law of Moses was given to people in a very low state of spiritual awareness, a very low state of spiritual consciousness. And because of that, they needed a very stern message!

To the first-century Jews, God was an object of worship, a male figure of authority who showed his presence on earth in altars, temples and synagogues, but resided permanently somewhere out there beyond the clouds, in the place known as heaven.

This was the God of Moses. A stern, unbending, unyielding deity, before whom all creatures trembled. A God of vengeance and wrath! A God who needed to be appeased by the continuous flow of blood from sacrificed animals. A God who was separate from mankind. A God who stipulated laws and exacted retribution for default. A God who condemned to hell for all eternity those who displeased him, and brought up into heaven with him for all eternity those who kept his laws.

Is this not all rather familiar? Is this not the way we too have been conditioned to think about God by the Christian churches? Is this not the teaching about God that dominates most Christian theology?

But as we shall see, this is most certainly not Jesus' concept of God!

In the Book of Numbers in the Old Testament we read about the punishment meted out to the man who broke the Sabbath:

"Once, while the Israelites were still in the wilderness, a man was found gathering firewood on the Sabbath. He was taken to Moses, Aaron, and the whole community, and was put under guard, because it was not clear what should be done with him. Then the Lord said to Moses, 'The man must be put to death; the whole community is to stone him to death outside the camp.' So the whole community took him outside the camp and stoned him to death, as the Lord had commanded." (Numbers 15: 32-36)

All rather extreme, don't you think? All rather excessive? All rather over-the-top?

Let us now move forwards through the centuries to the time of Jesus and see what he had to say about the same:

"Jesus was walking through some cornfields on the Sabbath. As his disciples walked along with him, they began to pick the ears of corn. So the Pharisees said to Jesus, 'Look, it is against our Law for your disciples to do that on the Sabbath!'

Jesus answered, 'Have you never read what David did that time when he needed something to eat? He and his men were hungry, so he went into the house of God and ate the bread offered to God. This happened when Abiathar was the High Priest. According to our Law, only the priests may eat this bread - but David ate it and even gave it to his men.'

And Jesus concluded, 'The Sabbath was made for the good of human beings; they were not made for the Sabbath. So the Son of Man is Lord even of the Sabbath.' " (Mark 2:23-28)

A big difference! No word of stoning or punishment of any kind with Jesus!

Let us take another example:

"You have heard that it was said, 'Love your friends, hate your enemies.' But now I tell you: love your enemies and pray for those who persecute you." (Matthew 5:43-44)

Those were the words of Jesus in the Sermon on the Mount. Contrast these with the words of Psalm 139 in the Old Testament where David says:

"I hate them with a total hatred; I regard them as my enemies." (Psalm 139:22-23)

"O God, how I wish you would kill the wicked." (Psalm 139:19)

and in Psalm 18:

"I pursue my enemies and capture them, I do not stop until I destroy them." (Psalm 18:37-38)

"I trample on them like mud in the streets." (Psalm 18:47)

See the difference?

Jesus' teachings must have raised many Jewish eyebrows!

Jesus' teachings must have perplexed many of those who listened!

And, of course, as we shall see, Jesus' teachings annoyed and angered many of those who listened!

Chapter 2
The Torah

What more do we know about Jewish beliefs?

Jewish beliefs and customs were totally embedded in the Torah.

The Torah is the central reference and the most important text of the religious Judaic tradition. The word "*Torah*" itself means "*instruction*" and the Torah consists of the historical narrative of the Jewish people, including their trials and tribulations, as well as a vast set of instructions concerning moral and religious obligations and civil laws.

The one and only God of the Jews was believed by them to have created the world and to be sovereign over the world and all forms of life in that world. They also believed that this one God chose them, the Jewish people, to be his special people, just as he was their special, one and only God.

God had proven to them just how special they were when he had delivered them from slavery in Egypt and brought them into the promised land, according to the instructions he issued to Moses in the Book of Exodus: "*Go and gather the leaders of Israel together and tell them that I, the Lord, the God of their ancestors, the God of Abraham, Isaac, and Jacob, appeared to you. Tell them that I have come to them and have seen what the Egyptians are doing to them. I have decided that I will bring them out of Egypt, where they are being treated cruelly , and will take them to a rich and fertile land.....* " (Exodus 3: 16-17)

God then delivered the Ten Commandments, the Law, to Moses on Mount Sinai (Exodus 20:1-17) together with laws about building altars, worship, offering animal sacrifices, the treatment of slaves, punishment for violent acts, instructions about justice and fairness, food, Sabbath observance, festivals and celebrations, and how to live with one another without strife.

Jews believed that God had given these laws to them to help them to know and live according to what was right and just. These laws were written down in the five books of Moses, known as Genesis, Exodus, Leviticus, Numbers and Deuteronomy.

Here was the Jewish Torah, which every Jewish child was taught from an early age. Also included in the Torah was the specific direction about circumcision, the outward sign that distinguished Jews and differentiated them from other religions and nations.

Then there were the instructions on food.

Meat was permitted, but only cattle and game that have '*divided hooves*' and '*chew the cud*'. (Deuteronomy 14: 6) In other words, bulls, cows, sheep, lambs, goats, veal were all permitted, while pork was forbidden. The Torah also specified that ritual slaughter had to be performed quickly and without delay, bringing instant death, to prevent unnecessary suffering to the animals.

Fish was permitted, but only fish with fins. Hence, shellfish, oysters, crabs, etc. were forbidden.

Specific instructions were given concerning the cooking of meat: "*Do not cook a young sheep or goat in its mother's milk*" and for the growing of crops: "*For six years sow your field and gather in what it produces. But in the seventh year let it rest, and do not harvest anything that grows on it. The poor may eat what grows there, and the wild animals can have what is left. Do the same with your vineyards and your olive trees".* (Exodus 23:10-11)

Further instructions included*: "If the one place of worship is too far away for you, then, whenever you wish, you may kill any of the cattle or sheep that the Lord has given you, and you may eat the meat at home ....only do not eat meat with blood still in it, for life is in the blood, and you must not eat the life with the meat. Do not use the blood for food; instead pour it out on the ground like water".* (Deuteronomy: 12:21)

Numerous and detailed instructions were given about the killing of animals as '*sin offerings*' and '*repayment offerings' (Leviticus: 6:24, 7:2)* and about '*grain offerings*' and how they should be presented at the Temple. (Leviticus 6: 14)

All in all, a mind-boggling number and variety of instructions with clear and detailed specifications!

The reasons for such specifications were never questioned by the Jewish people. It was good enough for them that the Torah said so, and they adhered to those teachings.

PART TWO: JESUS MAKING ENEMIES

Chapter 3

Life at the Temple and at the synagogues

The history of the Temple in Jerusalem is the history of the Jewish people themselves.

And if we want to understand Jesus' teachings, if we want to understand what he was trying to do, then we must first and foremost understand the happenings in the Temple and how Jewish people's lives centered entirely around this Temple.

Then, when we understand what Jesus was doing, we get a very different picture of Jesus from that depicted for us by orthodox religions!

Jesus came to earth 2,000 years ago, at a time when the earth consciousness was very dense, very limited, much more so than today. The teachings of Jesus were aimed at the limited consciousness of that time, and we must understand their beliefs if we are ever to understand Jesus' teachings.

Hence we must take a close look at what was going on in the Temple!

The site, Mount Moriah, or the Temple Mount, the highest point in Jerusalem, was chosen by King David, the second king of the united Kingdom of Israel and Judah, who ruled 1010-970 B.C.E. The reason for his particular choice was because that was believed to have been the spot where Abraham had built the altar on which to sacrifice his son Isaac.

That First Temple was built during the reign of David's son, King Solomon, and completed in 957 B.C.E. Other sanctuaries throughout the country retained their religious functions, but during the reign of Josiah, 640-609 B.C.E, these others were abolished and the Temple of Jerusalem was established as the only place of sacrifice in the entire Kingdom of Judah.

Solomon's Temple was built as a permanent abode for the Ark of the Covenant, believed to house God and the Ten Commandments, and which had previously been moved about from sanctuary to sanctuary, and finally brought to Jerusalem when David captured that city. The Temple building faced eastward, oblong in shape, and consisted of three rooms of equal width: the vestible or porch; the Holy Place or main room of religious service; and the Holy of Holies or sacred room which housed the Ark itself. There were five altars: a large tiered one in the courtyard; a large bronze one before the porch; two more inside the building; and finally, one at the entrance to the Holy of Holies. In the courtyard was a large bronze bowl filled with water, used for the priests' cleansing rituals. The Holy of Holies, held as the dwelling place of the Divine Presence, and therefore sacrosanct, could only be accessed by the high priest, and only once a year, on the Jewish festival of Yom Kippur or Day of Atonement, the '*day of purgation*'.

This First Temple, Solomon's Temple, was totally destroyed by the Babylonian King in 586 B.C.E, accompanying the deportation and exile of Jews into slavery in Babylon. This, however, was seen by the Jews as the fulfilment of prophecy, therefore strengthening Judaic religious beliefs and keeping alive their hopes for the future re-establishment of a Jewish independent state.

In 538 B.C.E. Babylon itself was conquered by the Persians, and the Jews were allowed to return to Jerusalem and rebuild the Temple.

This Second Temple was a modest version of the original First Temple, with courtyards and chambers, but without the Ark. In 169 B.C.E. the Temple was plundered by the Roman Antiochus IV Epiphanes who further desecrated it in 167 B.C.E. by commanding that sacrifices be offered to the god Zeus on an altar built especially for him. It was this that sparked off the Jewish Hasmonean revolt, during which one of the rebel leaders, Judas Maccabeus cleansed and rededicated the Temple, an event celebrated annually in the Jewish festival of Hannukkah.

In 63 B.C.E. the Roman Pompey Magnus, known as Pompey the Great, captured Jerusalem, extending the influence of the Romans over Judea. Pompey entered the Holy of Holies, but left the Temple itself intact. But in 54 B.C.E. the Roman general and governor of Roman Syria, Marcus Licinius Crassus plundered the Temple treasury.

It was during the reign of King Herod, Herod the Great, as he was known, 37 B.C.E. - 4 C.E. that the Second Temple was given a complete refurbishment. And it is here at this time that Jesus was born. This was the world into which he entered.

Herod was infatuated with Rome and with all things Roman. When he was made client King of Judea, he immediately set about developing and beautifying Jerusalem, attempting to create a new Rome in the Jewish city. A client King was a person appointed by Rome from within the conquered territory itself, to rule in the name of the Roman Empire. This system enabled Imperial Rome to flourish in all its conquered territories, the client king being from a local elite family, lavishly rewarded for his loyalty by prestigious titles and honours from Rome, and left mostly without interference to rule as he liked, just as long as he kept the country peaceful and kept the money collected from the exorbitant taxes pouring into the Roman coffers.

There was a problem with Herod, however. The Jewish people in Judea considered his claim to the Jewish kingship as illegitimate. He was only half-Jewish, his mother being an Arab, and therefore he was not of the pure blood believed necessary to qualify as the King of the Jews. Besides, his tribe, the Idumeans, had only been in Judea for a generation or so. The Jewish people did not therefore, consider Herod as in any way eligible for the Kingship. But Rome decided that Herod would be their king, and there was nothing they could do about it.

Herod began his lavish re-development programme in 20 B.C.E. He built towers, walls and palaces, amphitheatres, markets, public baths, wide colonnades and huge columns, all in the classical Hellenistic style. Greek became the established language of his court, and his coins were minted with Greek letters and insignia.

Three powerful towers were constructed into the old city walls, and adjoining these towers was Herod's own palace. At the northwest corner of the Temple area, a great fortress was built for the soldiers, and connected to the Temple porticos by two stairways or bridges, to enable the garrison positioned there to move swiftly to the Temple area when trouble arose. The fortress itself was named Antonia, after the Roman general Mark Antony, Herod's patron and the one who sponsored and furthered his claim as client King of Judea.

Herod also built fortresses, the best known of which was the fortress at Masada, the last strong-hold of the Jewish uprising, the first Jewish-Roman War, 66-73 C.E. where the remaining Jewish insurgents committed mass suicide rather than surrender to the Romans. It was after this, in 70 C.E. that Vespasian and his son Titus entered Jerusalem, raising it to the ground and completely destroying the Temple for the last time.

Herod was aware that he was not a popular choice as king for the Jewish people, and it was in great measure to curry favour and to ingratiate himself with his Jewish subjects that he began his refurbishment of the Temple in Jerusalem, which became known as the Temple of Herod. The rebuilding and refurbishment of the Temple took 80 years to complete and it was most probably Herod's most ambitious and most important architectural enterprise,

However, despite its magnificence, its opulence, its elegance, it lasted for only a short time, being raised to the ground and totally destroyed by Titus in 70 C. E. when the Romans entered the city during the Jewish uprising. Hence the prophecy of Jesus was fulfilled:

"As Jesus was leaving the Temple, one of his disciples said, 'Look, Teacher! What wonderful stones and buildings!' Jesus answered,

'You see these great buildings? Not a single stone here will be left in its place; every one of them will be thrown down.' " (Mark 13:1-2)

Titus reduced the immediate neighbourhood around Jerusalem to a vast wilderness. Josephus the first-century Jewish historian tells us how the city was so "*demolished it to its foundations, that nothing was left that could ever persuade visitors that it had once been a place of habitation."* Only the palace of Herod was retained, for administrative purposes.

But Herod's Temple had indeed been a remarkable edifice by any standards!

Herod had doubled the area of the Temple Mount and surrounded it all by a wall with gates, and the Temple itself was raised, enlarged and faced with white glittering stone, hard limestone, polished to make it sparkle in the hot sunlight and to be seen from all directions for miles around outside of Jerusalem. Of the retaining walls, the famous '*Wailing Wall'* still stands, a focal point of prayer for modern Jews, who have come to the wall for centuries to lament and mourn the destruction of the Temple, hence its name. On top of the new Temple, a golden eagle was erected, the symbol of Roman power, an obvious source of resentment by all the Jewish people. This was *their* Temple, and now it was desecrated by none other than the hated Romans!

But there was a further reason for such great resentment by the Jewish people against Herod and the Romans. The Roman takeover of the Jewish world was not the same as the Roman takeover of other parts of the Roman Empire for one main and irreconcilable difference. Jewish religion was not compatible with Roman beliefs and customs for the simple reason that while the Romans were polytheistic, believing in many gods, all for various purposes, Judaism was monotheistic, believing in and devoted to one god. An irreconcilable difference indeed!

So Herod certainly did not reconcile the Jewish people to Rome. He fell ill in 4 B.C.E. and during his illness, two popular teachers incited their students to remove the eagle from the Temple, following their teaching that according to the Ten Commandments, it was a sin to make idols. The teachers and their forty students were burned alive in reprisal.

After Herod's death in 4 B.C.E. the Kingdom was divided amongst his three sons, Herod Archelaus succeeding to Judea, the largest area, becoming the '*national leader* ', not client king, of Samaria and Judea. Now the country was split. Insurgents, no doubt inflamed and fuelled by the Jewish expectation of the imminent arrival of a Messiah to liberate them, and seething with anger, resentment and hatred, saw the change-over as a moment of potential weakness and seized their opportunity. A Zealot insurrection, led by Judas the Galilean, burned down what they could of Herod's and rampaged through the countryside, but they were ruthlessly crushed.

Under the hated Archelaus, messiahs sprang up, each declaring himself to be the one sent by God to deliver the Jewish people from the oppression of the hated Romans. These messianic aspirants were swiftly dealt with, usually publicly beheaded.

But let us now return to the Temple. The same Temple lavishly refurbished by Herod the Great, the hated King of the Jews.

The same Temple that Yeshua would have known well.

And why must we return to the Temple?

And what has all this got to do with finding the real Jesus?

Well, in a nutshell, as we shall see, this is what Jesus was trying to change!

Yes! Jesus was trying to change the way the Jewish people built their lives around the goings-on in the Temple. For them the Temple *was* their life.

So when Jesus tried to show them a better way to live, he was upsetting everything about their lives that they held dear.

And if Jesus was trying to change their way of life centered on the Temple, then there must have been something about that way of life that needed changing!

Hence our need to return to this same Temple.

Hence our need to take a closer look at what went on in this Temple in Jerusalem.

So now let us go back in time. Back 2,000 years ago. Back to first-century Jewish Palestine. Jerusalem to be exact. The Temple in Jerusalem to be specific.

Our mission? To find what it was about the goings-on in that Temple in Jerusalem that Jesus tried to change.

Let us enter the time capsule, travelling back in time, right back to first century Jewish Palestine. Leave behind all your pre-conceived ideas about life at that time. Leave behind all your 21st century ideas and beliefs.

Let us just observe!

Josephus, the first century Jewish historian tells us the Jews had "*One temple for the one God".* In the time of Jesus, this Jewish Temple, located of course in Jerusalem, was not just a building where Jews went to worship their God. This was the Temple embellished, extended and refurbished by Herod, built to be a show-piece. It was now a vast complex, a great array of tiered courtyards, all of varying sizes and all for different purposes. The Temple was the pivot, the centre, the focus of Jewish life. It was around the Temple and the elaborate, flamboyant ceremonies carried out there that the Jewish yearly calendar was organised. This was the venue for all kinds of activity, political, social, economic and religious, not just for the Jews living in Jerusalem itself, but also for those from the surrounding areas of Judea. As the chief commercial centre, daily activity included money transactions, legal transactions and buying and selling in all sorts of commercial activities.

And of course, it played a crucial, central role in the collective religious mentality of the Jewish people. For them, this was the one most sacred place on earth where God dwelled, where heaven and earth met, where their sins were washed away, where their culture, beliefs and values found expression and meaning.

Within the Temple compound, too, were the administrative

quarters of the Sanhedrin, the supreme religious body and highest judicial court of the Jewish nation, the body that met in the Hall of Hewn Stones. And here too, within this vast Temple complex, was the repository of the Holy Scriptures, the scrolls of law, legal documents, genealogical and other national records and literature.

It was in the Temple of Jerusalem only that sacrifices were permitted, hence Jews from all around the known world travelled to Jerusalem to join in the celebrations such as the Passover, held annually in March or April. This was an eight day barley festival, the celebration designated to commemorate the deliverance of the Jews from slavery in Egypt. There was therefore a political aspect to the festival of Passover, with a strong tone of national liberation. Dangerous! Needed to be watched carefully by the Roman authorities!

While the Passover, referred to as '*The Festival of Unleavened Bread*' (Matthew 26:17) was the biggest holiday that would bring in visitors from all over the known world, there were also two other pilgrimage festivals in Judaism, as described in the Bible. The festival of Yom Kippur, the Day of Atonement, was the holiest day in the Jewish year, a specific day when all the sins of the entire Jewish people would be washed away in the sacrificial blood of the slaughtered animals, and in the purification of the Temple, the land and the people. The festival of Hanukkah was an eight-day celebration held each year during winter to commemorate the joyful event of Judas Maccabeus cleansing and rededicating the Temple and Altar in 164 B.C.E. This festivity is referred to by John in 11:22 as '*The Dedication of the Temple'*, and it was on that occasion, in Solomon's porch that Jesus was questioned "*Are you the Messiah?"*

Ritual purity was a state necessary to partake in the festivals. Impurity was a state that was naturally assumed by Jewish Law, a natural state of being, as most impurity was seen to be tied to natural biological rhythms. Impurity was incurred by natural every-day living. Child-birth, sexual relations even with a marriage partner, menstrual cycle, having contact with a dead body, all would leave one in a state of impurity. So the elaborate rituals of cleansing and purification had to be gone through, with no exceptions. Water was the main means of purification, and the remains of what were huge immersion pools have been found by archaeologists in Jerusalem, at Masada, and throughout Galilee. Herod too, of course, in all his palaces, had his immersion pool for his ritual cleansing.

In order to perform this ritual cleansing, pilgrims frequently went to Jerusalem a week or so earlier before Passover actually started. Hence we see the crowd that accompanied Jesus into Jerusalem at the beginning of the week of Passover. Jesus, too, as well as the large numbers of people walking alongside him, was going to perform the ritual of cleansing in order to be in the proper, correct, holy state for the festival.

During these great festival periods, Jews from all across the Mediterranean areas, the Diaspora, flocked to Jerusalem and the Temple, the crowd sometimes swelling to over one million people. Roman troops usually stationed at the coast in Caesarea would be brought to Jerusalem for crowd control, as the huge numbers could easily get out of hand. The whole place thrived with noisy, excited activity, in the vast tiered courtyards, each area for a specific purpose, each representing a particular degree of sacred space and indeed, each for a particular class of people, the most sacred space occupied only by the priest. Pilgrims stayed in make-shift tents erected on the outskirts of the city, tent making being a common trade in first century Palestine. Indeed, Paul himself, of the New Testament writings, was a tent-maker by trade.

According to Josephus, there was the large outer court, commonly known as the Court of the Gentiles, Gentiles being all non-Jews. This included the vast numbers of Egyptians, Greeks, Romans and members of other nations resident in Jerusalem and in other parts of the country, and who travelled to Jerusalem for the great festivals. This great courtyard was theirs, and this was where they gathered to meet and socialise amongst the crowds.

Here too, the money changers changed the money of those who had travelled from other lands to attend the festival ceremonies, into the Hebrew shekel, the only currency accepted in the Temple. These money changers also made a lucrative package in the lending of credit to those who required it, in order to purchase their animal for the sacrificial offerings, and in the collecting of the half-shekel, which was the Temple tax levied on all male adults, for the upkeep of the Temple and the payment of those thousands of people who worked there, maintaining the continuous flow of sacrificial offerings and all the elaborate pomp and ceremony that went with it.

Next to this Court of the Gentiles and separated by a low wall, was the Court of the Israelites, into which no Gentile was permitted. On top of the wall, at regular intervals, were square stone pillars, each bearing an inscription in Greek forbidding any non-Jew to enter, under punishment of death.

After this outer court, divided into separate areas for Jews and Gentiles, there was a series of other courts, each leading further towards the centre, accessible only to people according to their cleanliness and worthiness, as specified in great detail by the Law of Moses. One could then progress further, up a series of terraced steps, up through the Women's Court and on up towards the main Temple area. Women, however, could progress no further than this Women's Court, because they were considered to be unclean most of the time, due to their menstrual cycle and child-birth. Men who were considered clean, those without infection or disease, and who had not recently been in contact with a dead body, could progress from the Women's Court upwards until finally, the Holy Chamber was reached.

It was probably around the Women's Court that Jesus did his teaching, or in the Court of the Gentiles, where most people would gather.

The Priest's Court, directly in front of the Temple edifice proper, was accessible only to the priests of the Temple, mostly the Levites, who served at all the great festivities. Here there was an altar upon which sacrifices and burnt offerings were made. There was a series of rings in the floor, where the animals about to be sacrificed were tethered. The carcasses were skinned, washed and prepared for the altar and the sacrificial fire on eight marble tables, from which a constant flow of blood poured. Here too, incense was burned and the people were blessed by those qualified to do so.

But the most revered, the most important place of all, was of course the Holy of Holies, the inner sanctuary within the Holy Place of the tabernacle, into which only the high priest himself was permitted, and even then, only on certain special days. Inside the Holy of Holies was an altar, complete with the Jewish seven-branched candlestick, in solid gold, and a light that was constantly kept lit. The walls of this inner sanctum were solid gold, everything lavishly adorned and decorated. This Holy of Holies was the most sacred room, a place where no ordinary person could enter. God dwelled in that room, and whoever entered into the Holy of Holies was entering the very presence of God.

A golden mirror hung above the entrance, reflecting the hot, shimmering rays of the sun, and then a veil kept everything else beyond the entrance from sight. This veil or curtain hid the gilded interior from ordinary lay men. Made of the finest linen, splendidly embroidered and decorated in blue, purple and scarlet yarn, with a zodiac wheel, images of the heavens and figures of angels embedded into it, it moved in the wind, creating a sparkling kaleidoscope of colour that shimmered in the sun. The cherubim embroidered on the veil demonstrated God's almighty power and majesty. These angelic beings were here in God's presence to serve Him and guard His throne.

This veil was seen as a barrier between man and God, shielding a holy God from sinful man. It showed that the holiness of God could not be trifled with. God's eyes are too pure to look on evil and He can tolerate no sin:

"B*ut how can you stand these treacherous evil men? Your eyes are too holy to look at evil and you cannot stand the sight of people* *doing wrong."* (Habakkuk 1: 13)

The veil was a barrier so that man could not carelessly and irreverently enter into God's awesome presence. This is the veil referred to in the gospels, which was rent in two when Jesus was crucified on the cross.

And, most importantly, it was torn from top to bottom! Only God himself could have done such a deed, as the veil was about 60 feet in height, 30 feet in width and 4 inches thick. The tearing must have been done from above, from God, and not by any mere mortal!

The early Christian church fathers attached much symbolism to the renting of that veil! It was proof for them that Jesus really was the Son of God! Even the Roman soldier at the cross acknowledged this, according to the gospels! The Holy of Holies is a representation of heaven itself, God's dwelling place. As the veil was torn, the Holy of Holies was exposed for the first time to all men, making God's presence accessible to everyone. The age of animal offerings to appease an angry God and to atone for man's sins was ended. The high priest no longer had to enter the Holy of Holies every year with blood. Jesus' sacrifice on the cross had been accepted in atonement for the sins of all mankind, past, present and future. The ultimate offering! The ultimate sacrifice! The ultimate atonement!

So, as we have seen, at the centre of it all, of paramount importance, was the ceremony of the sacrificial offerings, a ceremony conducted within this *Holy of Holies,* the very centre of the temple complex, into which only the high priest was permitted.

The high priest who had purchased his lucrative, elevated and revered position from Rome, and who could, therefore, be totally relied upon to act in accordance with Roman wishes!

There was a strict hierarchy amongst those who served in the Temple. At the top of this prestigious pile was of course the high priest with other priests serving under him, performing the more manual tasks such as the constant cleaning of the Temple grounds. It was the priests, but most of all the high priest who exhibited the most opulence and lavishness.

So now let us look closer at this high priest and his role in the Temple.

The high priest was the chief religious official of Judaism from early times right up to the destruction of the Jewish Temple by Titus in 70 C.E. The title *High Priest* was accompanied by great religious and political significance.

The first high priest of Israel was Aaron, the elder brother of Moses. According to Exodus, God himself had appointed Aaron to the position in his instructions to Moses:

"*Summon your brother Aaron and his sons, Nadab, Abihu, Eleazar, and Ithamar. Separate them from the people of Israel, so that they may serve me as priests.*" (Exodus 28: 1-2)

"Bring Aaron and his sons to the entrance of the Tent of my presence, and tell them to take a ritual bath. Then dress Aaron in the priestly garments.......put the turban on him and tie on it the sacred sign of dedication engraved 'Dedicated to the Lord'. Then take the anointing oil, pour it on his head, and anoint him." (Exodus 29:4-7)

Succeeding high priests from that time could trace their paternal line back to Aaron through Zadok, a leading priest at the time of

David and Solomon. This tradition, however, ended in the second century B.C.E. during the rule of the Hasmodians, when the position of high priest was occupied by other priestly families, at the instigation of Roman authorities.

Herod the Great nominated no less than six high priests, and his successor, his son Archelaus, two.

From this time onwards, the Temple became not only the symbol of the Jewish nation, but also the symbol of collaboration with Rome. The high priests were appointed by Rome and their allegiance was henceforth to Rome first before the Jewish people. They came to be seen as a fawning bunch who valued their privileged position and all the wealth and prestige that came with it.

The Torah, and in particular, Exodus, Deuteronomy and Leviticus all specified very clearly the attire to be worn by the high priest when he was ministering at the Temple:

"Make priestly garments for your brother Aaron, to provide him with dignity and beauty...........call all the skilled workers to whom I have given ability.........the skilled workers are to use blue, purple, and red wool, gold thread, and fine linen......decorated with embroidery.....take two carnelian stones and engrave on them the names of the twelve sons of Jacob.......get a skilled jeweller to engrave on the two stones the names of the sons of Jacob, and mount the stones in gold settings. Put them on the shoulder straps of the ephod to represent the twelve tribes of Israel. In this way Aaron will carry their names on his shoulders, so that I, the Lord, will always remember my people. Make two gold settings, and two chains of pure gold twisted like cords, and attach them to the settings...........make an ornament of pure gold and engrave on it 'Dedicated to the Lord'. Tie it to the front of the turban with a blue cord. Aaron is to wear it on his forehead, so that I, the Lord, will accept all the offerings that the Israelites dedicate to me..........."
(Exodus 28)

In all, the high priest wore eight holy garments, four of which were also worn by the other priests. Of these, there were the undergarments, the breeches, linen pants reaching from the waist to the knees, *"so that they will not expose themselves".* (Exodus 28:42) Then there was the priestly tunic, made of pure linen, covering the entire body from the neck to the feet, with sleeves reaching to the wrists. Those of the priests were plain, while the high priest's was embroidered. There was also a sash. The high priest's was "*decorated with embroidery*" and made of "*fine linen and of blue, purple, and red wool*" (Exodus 28:39)

The ephod was unique to the high priest. Under the ephod was a sleeveless, blue robe, *"made entirely of blue wool. The hole for the head was reinforced with a woven binding to keep it from tearing. All around its lower hem they put pomegranates of fine linen and of blue, purple, and red wool, alternating with bells of pure gold, just as the Lord had commanded Moses".* (Exodus 39:22) The ephod itself was a richly embroidered apron with two onyx engraved gemstones on the shoulders. "*They hammered out sheets of gold and cut them into thin strips to be worked into the blue, purple, and red wool.*" (Exodus 39: 2-21)

The priestly garments certainly were a central part of all the Temple happenings, the vast numbers of priests and the high priest himself creating a spectacular scene of colour and light as they sauntered along, the sun blazing and shimmering off their elaborate gold vestments and their gold and coloured baubles and bells bobbing and bouncing.

The high priest, like all priests, would be barefoot while ministering at the Temple. All of them had to purify and cleanse themselves by immersing in the ritual bath before adorning themselves in the vestments, and wash their hands and feet before performing any sacred act.

The high priest could enter the Holy of Holies, pass through the veil only one day out of every year, on the Day of Atonement. Before entering, he had to make some meticulous preparations, as recorded in Leviticus:

"The Lord spoke to Moses.......... Tell your brother Aaron that only at the proper time is he to go behind the curtain into the Most Holy Place, because that is where I appear in a cloud above the lid on the Covenant Box. If he disobeys, he will be killed. He may enter the Most Holy Place only after he had brought a young bull for a sin offering and a ram for a burnt offering.

*Then the Lord gave the following instructions. Before Aaron goes inti the Most Holy Place, he must have a bath and put on the priestly garments: the linen robe and shorts, the belt, and the turban." (*Leviticus 16:2-19)

There follows in Leviticus further detailed and precise instructions for cleansing the altar, and the whole interior of this Most Holy Place before the actual sacrificial ritual could even begin.

So the high priest had to wash himself, put on special clothing, bring burning incense to let the smoke cover his eyes from a direct view of God, because, as it was believed God said to Moses:

'I will not let you see my face because no one can see me and stay alive.' (Exodus 33:20)

He had to bring the blood of animals with him to atone for the sins of himself and the nation of Israel. If he did not bring blood, he would not be acceptable before God because of his sins. He would be guilty and would die in God's presence. A rope was attached to his waist in case he did die, and then he could be ceremoniously hauled out without anyone else seeing the face of God or defiling God's inner sanctum.

All very theatrical and dramatic!

The actual sacrificing of the animals and all it entailed was big business. The animals were reared especially for that purpose, none of them being domestic animals, and they came at a price to meet all pockets. They were purchased in the temple complex, and then collected by the thousands of white-robed priests who had flocked to Jerusalem to assist, and brought to the high priest for instant slaughter. The Torah demanded continuous ongoing sacrificial offerings, all of which were believed to protect from disasters such as famine, drought or earthquakes, appeasing an angry god and wiping away the sins of the purchaser. There was a constant stream of people going to the Temple to offer sacrifice in thanksgiving for a new baby, a child or relative delivered from an illness, or to make various requests for favours. On the feast of Yom Kippur, the Jewish Day of Atonement, it was believed that all the sins of the entire Israelite nation would be wiped away. The slate was completely cleaned!

This continuous burning of sacrificial animals was, of course, accompanied by the most awful, nauseating stench, and the black billowing smoke that hung over everything. Hence the lavish burning of incense such as cinnamon, saffron, frankincense and myrrh. The animal's throat was swiftly slit, the entrails ripped out and piled on the sacrificial fire. The hide was retained by the priests to sell for the best price at a later transaction, and the meat itself was reserved for a later feast by the priests.

The amount of blood spilled was so great that the Temple in Jerusalem had gutters built into the stone floor around the altar, into which flowed the blood of all these hundreds and thousands of sheep, cows, goats and fowl that were sacrificed on a constant daily basis to appease the Jewish god. Rivers of blood, literally, flowed from the Temple.

And of course, all this lavish splendour, all these spectacular, flamboyant displays and ceremonies had to be paid for! And the lavish, opulent life-styles of those who performed an these continuous spectacular ceremonial occasions had to be paid for!

So it is not difficult to see how so much hatred and resentment was generated among the population by the high priest and priests of the temple! Those described by Josephus as greedy '*lovers of luxury*'.

Their extremely lucrative positions, their subservience to Roman authorities, the opulence, the pomp and ceremony, together with the expensive upkeep and payment of thousands of porters, servants, singers, all part and parcel of the daily goings on in the temple, were all paid for by the ordinary person, whose sole aim was simply to fulfil the command of the Torah, which required constant daily sacrificial offerings, but which provided such a lucrative income for so many detested people. People whose allegiance was obviously to the Roman authorities, to whom they owed their positions.

So, we have seen life in the Temple in Jesus' own day.

Jesus himself taught in the Temple, as we see many times in the gospels.

He would have stood probably in the Court of the Gentiles or around the Women's Court, under the columns and porticoes, as those were the areas to which everyone had access.

We have seen how the Jewish people centered their entire lives around the Temple and the festivities going on there. We have seen the elaborate preparation rituals and ceremonies, with all the cleansings and purifications, ritual purity and sacredness.

We have seen the way in which people were divided up into different sections and categories, according not only to race and gender, but also according to various degrees of worthiness and cleanliness, with only the elite and the purest allowed to the highest levels in the Temple.

We have seen the brutal sacrificial offerings and the constant sea of blood that flowed from the Most Holy Place.

We have seen the elaborate costumes and finery worn by the priests and especially the high priest during these elaborate ceremonies to appease an angry God.

We have seen how the high priest took on the role of intermediary between the people and God, he being the only one allowed into God's presence, the only with direct access to God, everyone else deprived of direct contact.

We have seen the arrogance and pomposity of the high priest, puffed up with his own importance and sense of superiority, a spectacular bejewelled mirage, sparkling and shimmering, glowing and glimmering in his magnificent array, his lavish vestments flowing in the breeze in a kaleidoscopic extravaganza of colour and magnificence, as he strutted his way across the Court of Priests, luxuriating in the adoration of the masses, before ceremoniously entering the Holy of Holies, before the huge, awe-struck crowds of people thronging the vast tiered courtyards below him. The only one who could remove their sins; the only one who could intercede with God on their behalf; the only one on earth who had the power to open the gates of heaven or close the gates of hell for them.

We have seen the money that was needed to keep the Temple functioning, money that was exacted from the Jewish people already severely suffering under a heavy taxation system imposed by Rome.

We have seen how that money supported lavish life-styles for the priests and the high priest, and paid all others who served in the Temple.

We have seen the elaborate outward displays of magnificence and opulence, the outward displays of pomp and spectacular ceremony, the outward displays of sacrificial offerings, offerings that would redeem man's sins and gain forgiveness from a punishing, admonishing God.

This was the way in which the Jewish people saw and paid homage to their God!

This was how the Jewish people lived their lives!

And it was this that Jesus tried to change!

Yes! It was this Temple set-up, with all its strict rituals, its opulence, all its splendid costumes, all its brutal sacrificial offerings, all its transparent holiness and sacredness, all its flamboyancy and mercenary dealings, that Jesus was attempting to transform!

And that was why he so angrily cleared the Temple!

"When they arrived in Jerusalem, Jesus went to the Temple and began to drive out all those who were buying and selling. He overturned the tables of the money-changers and the stools of those who sold pigeons, and he would not let anyone carry anything through the Temple courtyards. He then taught the people: 'It is written in the Scriptures that God said, 'My Temple will be called a house of prayer for the people of all nations. But you have turned it into a hideout for thieves.' " (Mark 11:15-17)

Even though Jesus too was a Jew, his views were different. Jesus did not attach the same importance to the various stages of holiness that his pious contemporaries did. He felt they were preoccupied by focusing on the ritual and the ceremony, rather than what these stood for. They had forgotten the individual person and his needs. They thought that their sins could be wiped away by the sacrificial blood of animals.

Jesus tried to change them from outward displays of fake holiness to looking inwards, into themselves, to find God.

Jesus tried to show them that all men are equal, that God is not only accessible to everyone, but lies within everyone. There is no need for intermediaries to intercede on people's behalf.

Jesus tried to show them that no amount of blood sacrifice will gain pardon for sins. Repentance is the responsibility of every individual.

Jesus tried to show them that God is not an external force, a male figure somewhere up in the skies, watching and waiting for us to stumble.

No wonder he came into conflict with those who served in the Temple, and with the entire Jewish people! He was standing against, criticising, their very way of life! Calling it for what it was! A mere mockery! A mere outward show to appease an angry God!

Jesus was repeatedly rebuking the religious authorities of his time. He was repeatedly rebuking those who set themselves up as the only gateway between humanity and God. He was repeatedly rebuking those who taught that the only road to salvation was through an outer organisation and outer dogmas and doctrines.

Many of Jesus' teachings centered around the Temple:

"*As Jesus sat near the Temple treasury, he watched the people as they dropped in their money. Many rich men dropped in a lot of money; then a poor widow came along and dropped in two little copper coins, worth about a penny. He called his disciples together and said to them, 'I tell you that this poor widow put more in the offering box than all the others. For the others put in what they had to spare of their riches, but she, poor as she is, put in all she had - she gave all she had to live on.*'" (Mark 12: 41-44)

And, of course, the famous parable of the Good Samaritan. What was Jesus trying to do here?

"There was once a man who was going down from Jerusalem to Jericho when robbers attacked him, stripped him and beat him up, leaving him half dead. It so happened that a priest was going down

that road, but when he saw the man, he walked on by, on the other side. In the same way, a Levite also came along, went over and looked at the man, and then walked on the other side. But a Samaritan who was travelling that way, came upon the man, and when he saw him, his heart was filled with pity. He went over to him, poured oil and water on his wounds and bandaged them; then he put the man on his own animal and took him to an inn, where he took care of him." (Luke 10: 31-34)

If we examine this parable closely, we will see that it has been misrepresented to us. The Samaritans were considered by the Jews to be the lowliest, most impure class of people, simply because they did not recognise the supremacy of the Temple of Jerusalem or that Temple as being the sole place of worship. They worshipped instead in their own temple on Mount Gerizim, on the western bank of the River Jordan.

In the parable, the Samaritan, who denies the authority of the Temple, goes out of his way to help the man, while the priests, including the Levite, ignore the suffering man completely, for fear of defiling their racial purity.

So who exactly is Jesus criticising here?

Jesus is very clearly criticising the priests of the temple! It is certainly the anti-clerical sentiments of Jesus that dominate this parable!

So yes! It is very obvious that it was the Temple system that Jesus was trying to reform and change!

Jesus was directing his criticism at those who had created a belief system that no human being could get to God except through the orthodox religion and its closed-minded hierarchy of human beings.

But in doing so, he made too many enemies! Too many enemies from those who were gaining from the Temple system, earning a lucrative living from it! Those religious authorities who considered him too much of a threat that they repeatedly sought to kill him. Jesus was the ultimate threat to their power structure.

And remember how he cleared the Temple?

"When they arrived in Jerusalem, Jesus went to the Temple and began to drive out all those who were buying and selling. He overturned the tables of the money-changers and the stools of those who sold pigeons, and he would not let anyone carry anything through the Temple courtyards. He then taught the people: 'It is written in the Scriptures that God said, 'My Temple will be called a house of prayer for the people of all nations, but you have turned it in to a hideout for thieves!' " (Mark 11:15-17)

Harsh words indeed!

And after he cleared the Temple:

"The chief priests and the teachers of the Law heard of this, so they began looking for some way to kill Jesus. They were afraid of him, because the whole crowd was amazed at his teaching." (Mark 11:18-19)

Dangerous thing to make enemies of the priests of the Temple or the religious authorities! Could cost you your life! As it certainly did for Jesus!

As it has certainly done for millions of people over the last 2,000 years who dared to question or oppose the teachings of the Church!

And what about the synagogues? What was the difference between what went on in the synagogues and what went on in the Temple in Jerusalem?

Well, firstly, while there was only one Temple, the Temple in Jerusalem, there were numerous synagogues.

Outside of Jerusalem, every small town or village had its own synagogue. Jews gathered in the synagogues, especially and particularly on the Sabbath, the day of rest, where, instead of worshipping through offerings of blood sacrifices, they listened to readings of the Torah and discussed sacred scriptures. Prolific debates and renderings of interpretations took place regularly, with wide-ranging differences voiced and considered. Jesus regularly preached and taught in the various synagogues, as related in the gospels:

"Jesus went all over Galilee, teaching in the synagogues, preaching the Good News about the Kingdom, and healing people who had all kinds of disease and sickness." (Matthew 4:23)

"Jesus and his disciples came to the town of Capernaum, and on the next Sabbath Jesus went to the synagogue and began to teach. The people who heard him were amazed at the way he taught, for he wasn't like the teachers of the Law. Instead, he taught with authority." (Mark 1:21)

It was in the synagogue too that Jesus healed the man with the paralysed hand (Mark 3:1), and it was also in the synagogue of Nazareth, his own home place that the people rejected him. (Mark 6:1)

The local synagogue was part and parcel of the Jewish lifestyle, even before the destruction of the Temple. The synagogue was for reading the Torah and the Prophets, studying the commandments, teaching and hosting visitors from abroad. After the sacred Temple was destroyed in 70 C.E. the synagogue became the central focus for worship and prayer.

Jesus' pattern of visiting the synagogue and preaching in it was entirely consistent with the pattern of sectarian preachers or teachers common in his day. Like Yeshua, these preachers also had disciples.

But, unlike these preachers, Jesus' message has touched nearly every nation, which of course is a good thing. However, in the process, the nature and identity of the Messiah has been tampered with, even altered, by those without the authority to do so. Yeshua has been divorced from his Jewish identity in the eyes of the world at large. His teachings became steeped in Gentile culture, foreign to the Jewish people.

So, first of all, Jesus made enemies with the priests of the Temple and the religious authorities, as we have just seen. Jesus was intent on destroying that old closed system, abolishing for good that dogmatic, dictatorial regime that kept men in bondage to outward doctrines and dogmas.

But he also made enemies of other sections of Jewish society through his teachings.

He made enemies of the Pharisees and Sadducees, the two major, most important sects!

Let us now take a close look at these two sects and see what Jesus did to annoy them.

Let us take a closer look at what Jesus was teaching that annoyed these Pharisees and Sadducees so much that it eventually cost him his life!

Chapter 4

Pharisees and Sadducees

According to Josephus, the first-century Jewish historian, the Pharisees and the Sadducees were the two main sects in Jewish society in first-century Jewish Palestine, and they are very familiar to us from the gospels.

We saw in the last chapter how Jesus antagonised the priests of the Temple and brought their wrath down upon himself.

But not just the priests of the Temple! Jesus also managed to antagonise both the Pharisees and the Sadducees!

And how did he manage to do that?

Again, through his teachings!

So let us now take a closer look at these two very different sects and see how Jesus came into conflict with each of them.

The Pharisees

Josephus tells us: "*Now the Pharisees simplify their way of life and give into no sort of softness; and they follow the guidance of what their doctrine has handed down and prescribes as good; and they earnestly strive to observe the commandments it dictates to them. They also show respect to the elders, nor are they so bold as to contradict them in any thing they have introduced. Although they determine that all things are done by fate, they do not take away the freedom from men as acting as they think fit; since it has pleased God to make a combination of his council-chamber and of the people who wish to approach with their virtue and their vice. They also believe that souls have an immortal power in them, and that under the earth there will be rewards or punishments according to whether they showed virtue or vice in this life; the latter are to be detained in an everlasting prison, but the former are allowed an easy passage through and live again. Because of these doctrines they hold great influence among the populace, and all divine worship, prayers, and sacrifices are performed according to their direction. In doing so the cities bear witness to their virtuous conduct, both in their way of life and in their words."* (*'Antiquities'* 18.1.2-3)

However, in the Gospel of Matthew we see a different view of the Pharisees when we read how Jesus spoke to the crowds and to his disciples: "*The teachers of the Law and the Pharisees are the authorized interpreters of Moses' Law. So you must obey and follow everything they tell you to do; do not, however, imitate their actions, because they don't practise what they preach.......they do everything so that people will see them.........they love the best places at feasts and the reserved seats in the synagogues. They love to be greeted with respect and to be called Teacher.*" (Matthew 23:2-7)

Addressing the Pharisees themselves, Jesus calls them: "*You hypocrites! ....Blind guides!....... Blind fools!..........You clean the outside of your cup and plate, while the inside is full of what you have obtained by violence and selfishness..........you are like whitewashed tombs.... on the outside you appear good to everybody, but inside you are full of hypocrisy and sins."* (Matthew 23: 13-28)

This is how most Christians tend to see the Pharisees,- as hypocrites!

Luke furthers this impression: "*How terrible for you teachers of the Law! You have kept the key that opens the door to the house of knowledge; you yourselves will not go in, and you stop those who are trying to go in!"* (Luke 11:52)

As does Mark:

"A large crowd was listening to Jesus gladly. As he taught them, he said, 'Watch out for the teachers of the Law, who like to walk around in their long robes, and be greeted with respect in the market place, who choose the reserved seats in the synagogues and the best places at feasts. They take advantage of widows and rob them of their homes, and then make a show of saying long prayers. Their punishment will be all the worse!" (Mark 12:38-40)

What Josephus and Matthew do agree upon though, is the dependence the people had on the Pharisees to instruct them in doctrine.

Whatever way we see them, the Pharisees were a highly religious group who emphasised the importance of keeping the Law given to them by God. They were members of Jewish middle class families who were committed to upholding the Law of Moses. That Law however, was very vague and unclear in the instructions as to how exactly one should obey the Law, and so this gave rise to lots of arguments, questioning, debate and discussion, for which the Pharisees were noted, all aimed at identifying the best way for people to keep the Law. It was all about the Law for them and adherence to the Law.

"Even then, many of the Jewish authorities believed in Jesus; but because of the Pharisees they did not talk about it openly so as not to be expelled from the synagogue. They loved human approval rather than the approval of God." (John 12:42-43)

We see throughout the gospels how Jesus was constantly in conflict with the Pharisees over their intent and over-concern about keeping the Law, for example in observing the Law of rest on the Sabbath, but disagreements and conflict were part of every day life amongst all the different and various sects in Judaism.

Matthew *tells us: "The Pharisees went off and made a plan to trap Jesus with questions".* (Matthew 22:15)

And again: *"When the Pharisees heard that Jesus had silenced the Sadducees, they came together, and one of them, a teacher of the law, tried to trap him with a question. 'Teacher', he asked, 'which is the greatest commandment in the Law?'* (Matthew 22: 34-36)

In Luke's Gospel, we read: "*One Sabbath Jesus went to eat a meal at the home of one of the leading Pharisees; and people were watching Jesus closely. A man whose legs and arms were swollen came to Jesus, and Jesus asked the teachers of the Law and the Pharisees , 'Does our Law allow healing on the Sabbath or not?'*

But they would not say anything. Jesus took the man, healed him, and then sent him away. Then he said to them, 'If any one of you had a son or an ox that happened to fall into a well on a Sabbath, would you not pull them out at once on the Sabbath itself?'

But they were not able to answer him about this." (Luke 14:1-6)

In Matthew's Gospel: *"When some Pharisees gathered together, Jesus asked them, 'What do you think about the Messiah? Whose descendant is he?'*

'He is David's descendant', they answered.

'Why then ' Jesus asked, 'did the Spirit inspire David to call him 'Lord'? David said: 'The Lord said to my Lord: Sit here on my right until I put your enemies under your feet.' If, then, David called him 'Lord', how can the Messiah be David's descendant?'

No one was able to give Jesus any answer, and from that day on, no one dared to ask him any more questions." (Matthew:22:41-45)

So now we see that Jesus was in constant conflict with the Pharisees because of their adherence to, and obsession with the Laws, all just on the outside. Hypocrites he called them!

Even when he was dying on the cross:

"*The chief priests and the teachers of the Law and the elders jeered at him."* (Matthew 27:41)

"There was a Jewish leader named Nicodemus, who belonged to the party of the Pharisees. One night he went to Jesus and said to

him, 'Rabbi, we know that you are a teacher sent by God. No one could perform the miracles you are doing unless God were with him.'

Jesus answered,

I am telling you the truth: no one can see the Kingdom of God without being born again.'

'How can a grown man be born again?' Nicodemus asked. 'He certainly cannot enter his mother's womb and be born a second time!'

'I am telling you the truth', replied Jesus. 'No one can enter the Kingdom of God without being born of water and the Spirit. A Person is born physically of human parents but is born spiritually of the Spirit. Do not be surprised because I tell you that you must all be born again. The wind blows wherever it wishes; you hear the sound it makes, but you do not know where it comes from or where it is going. It is like that with everyone who is born of the Spirit.'

'How can this be?' answered Nicodemus.

Jesus answered, 'You are a great teacher in Israel, and you don't know this? I am telling you the truth: we speak of what we know and report what we have seen, yet none of you is willing to accept our message. You do not believe me when I tell you about the things of this world; how will you ever believe me then, when I tell you about the things of heaven?' " (John 3:1-13)

He was in conflict with the priests of the Temple, now the Pharisees! Because of their outward display of strict adherence to the Law and their knowledge of that Law, with no inner vision or understanding of what any of it all meant. Just keeping the Law was, they believed, sufficient for them to get to heaven and they were content with that. Jesus repeatedly rebuked those who learned and kept the outer doctrines and teachings, yet never attempted to reach an inner understanding of those same teachings. The outer teachings are merely a stepping stone to understanding the inner teachings. But they believed that if they kept the law they would be saved, if they broke the law they would be lost.

But that was not what Jesus taught! Jesus taught that the kingdom of heaven is within and only from within oneself can one find God.

But the Pharisees believed in an external God, punishing, admonishing, condemning.

This was not what Jesus taught!

Let us now see how he fared with the Sadducees!

The Sadducees

The Sadducees were very different from the Pharisees. In fact, probably the best way to describe the Sadducees is to say they were the direct opposite of the Pharisees!

While the Pharisees were mostly lower and middle class, the Sadducees were members of the Jewish aristocracy. While the Pharisees were the teachers of the Law, rabbis and scholars, interpreting the laws for the people, the Sadducees were involved chiefly with the sacrificial ceremonies at the temple, most of them operating as priests. While the Pharisees, as we have just noted, believed in heaven and hell, the Sadducees did not believe that man would experience resurrection after physical death.

It was this latter that was the chief cause of disagreement.

In Acts, Luke tells us*: "For the Sadducees say that people will not rise from death and that there are no angels or spirits; but the Pharisees believe in all three."* (Acts: 23:8)

There were always arguments and disagreements going on between these two sects, each one in opposition to the other.

*"Then some Sadducees, who say that people will not rise from death, came to Jesus."(*Mark 12:18)

"That same day some Sadducees came to Jesus and claimed that people will not rise from death." (Matthew 22: 23)

"Then some Sadducees, who say that people will not rise from death, came to Jesus." (Luke 20:27)

"Peter and John were still speaking to the people when some priests, the officer in charge of the temple guards, and some Sadducees arrived. They were annoyed because the two apostles were teaching the people that Jesus had risen from death, which proved that the dead will rise to life". (Acts: 4:1-2)

Josephus writes: "*But the doctrine of the Sadducees is that souls die with the bodies. Nor do they perform any observance other than what the Law enjoins them. They think it virtuous to dispute with the teachers of the wisdom they pursue. This doctrine is accepted but by a few, but those are of the highest standing. But they are able to accomplish almost nothing, for when they hold office they are unwillingly and by force obliged to submit to the teachings of the Pharisees, because the multitude would not otherwise tolerate them.*" (Antiquities 18.2.4 16-17)

Matthew*: "That same day some Sadducees came to Jesus* and

claimed the people will not rise from death. 'Teacher', they said, 'Moses said that if a man who has no children dies, his brother must marry the widow so that they can have children who will be considered the dead man's children.' (Matthew 22: 23-24)

As we have seen earlier, the priests of the temple were the ones whose task it was to carry out the continuous daily sacrificial ceremonies including the rapid slaughter of the sacrificial animals, demanded in the Torah.

The Sadducean High Priest was the one who held the highest power, being the chief liaison with the ruling Roman authorities, on whom they all realised full well they were dependent for their positions and privileges, and so the Sadducees were pro-Roman and tended to tow the line as far as the Romans were concerned.

The Sadducees were also the main ones who comprised the Sanhedrin. This was the local Jewish council, composed of 70 elders and the High Priest, who had control of religious affairs. They also administered government and justice under the authority of the Roman procurator. They did not have the right, however, to enforce capital punishment, and that was why Jesus had to be condemned by Pontius Pilate, the Roman governor.

We read in the gospels how Jesus came into conflict with the Sadducees over his opposition to the Temple, the sacrifices offered there and the ceremonies performed.

"Jesus went into the temple and drove out all who were buying and selling there. He overturned the tables of the moneychangers and the stools of those who sold pigeons and said to them, 'It is written in the Scriptures that God said, 'My Temple will be called a house of

prayer, but you are making it a hideout for thieves." (Matthew 21:12-13)

"Jesus came to the Temple; as he taught, the chief priests and the elders came to him and asked, 'What right have you to do these things? Who gave you the right?' " (Matthew 21:23)

"The chief priests and the teachers of the Law became angry when they saw the wonderful things he was doing". (Matthew 21: 15)

In expressing his strong opposition, Jesus brought on himself the wrath of the local ruling authorities, the Sadducees, and they certainly played a key role in Jesus being turned over to the Roman governor, Pontius Pilate, who was in Jerusalem to keep the peace during the unsettling and disturbing days of the Jewish Passover festival.

So, Jesus clearly antagonised not only the priests and rulers of the Temple, but also, as we have just seen, the Pharisees, and now the Sadducees!

Jesus took every opportunity he could get to expose both the Pharisees and the Sadducees, especially in public, in full hearing of the crowds, accusing them of jostling for the place of honour at the feasts or in the synagogues, of stealing from widows, and of parading themselves in public looking for admiration and commendation.

And not only that!

Jesus called them names, as we have seen, and very insulting names at that!

Insulting names such as "*hypocrites......snakes........a brood of vipers..... whited sepulchres.....blind fools.*"

In fact, it would not be an exaggeration to say that Jesus went so far as to actually provoke them!

And also, of course, we cannot forget how he wrecked the Temple!

Not by any means the most tactful or diplomatic of actions!

Now let me ask you a question!

If you were to meet Jesus and you were allowed to ask him one question, just one question, what would your question be? Do you know?

I certainly know what my question, my one allowed question would be!

I would ask Jesus what exactly did he think he was at? What did he think he was doing provoking the priests at the Temple, provoking the Pharisees, provoking the Sadducees and provoking the Jewish authorities? And not inadvertently provoking them! But deliberately provoking them!

Was he on some sort of suicide mission? Some sort of self-destruct path? Some sort of death wish?

This is what I attempt to answer for the reader in my next book, '*Jesus: Lost and found*'. But for the moment, just let us see and acknowledge that Jesus came to expose the power structures in his time, and to overthrow those power structures.

And not only that!

Not only did Jesus aim to expose the power structures and the power plays, but more importantly, he aimed to expose the power players. Those who played and toyed with people's lives in their bid to achieve control over the population. Those who exerted control by teaching outer doctrines, and creating the belief system that only outer doctrines and dogmas can lead one to salvation.

Jesus' teachings were unique, based on love, in sharp contrast to the teachings of the Jewish religion of his time, which emphasised justice, the law, knowledge and power.

And when Jesus associated with criminals and prostitutes and those whom the religious authorities regarded as impure and unclean, the very lowest of the low, he was flouting all the conventions of Jewish society.

And when he extended his teachings right down through the social ranks to the poorest and the uneducated, he angered those closed, narrow-minded authorities even further.

And so he made himself unacceptable to those who were determined to retain the established existing order.

And it cost him his life!

PART THREE: TRUE INNER TEACHINGS OF JESUS

Chapter 5

Jesus the Teacher

Jesus was the Master Teacher. His teachings were a combination of the '*Esoteric*' and the '*Exoteric*', and we need to understand these two very different terms if we are ever going to understand Jesus and his teachings.

So what is the difference between esoteric teachings and exoteric teachings?

Exoteric means the '*outer*', in the sense of being on the surface, the ordinary understandings, everyday consciousness, everyday awareness with no hidden meaning attached.

Esoteric, on the other hand, means the '*inner*', in the sense of the inner consciousness, the meditative, mystical or contemplative perspective. This is different from the ordinary everyday understanding of things, and so can only be understood by intuition or higher or spiritual faculties. Esoteric teachings and understanding require an altered state of consciousness, a deep spiritual connection, beyond the basic everyday surface understanding of things, unlike exoteric understanding which does not require a shift in consciousness.

So '*states of consciousness*' is central to the distinction between esoteric and exoteric understanding. We need to raise our spiritual consciousness to move from the exoteric to the esoteric, from the outer to the inner.

And why do we need to move from the exoteric to the esoteric? From the outer to the inner?

Simply because we cannot know God or the spiritual truths through outer knowledge only, through the exoteric. It is only through the esoteric, the inner experience within ourselves that we can connect with God or with Jesus.

We must go beyond the limited consciousness of the five physical senses and experience through our inner spiritual chakra sensory system.

An exoteric religion or philosophy is one which is based on external factors and teachings, outside of the individual, and on the normal everyday state of consciousness, which we experience naturally during our waking hours. Such a religion teaches that power lies outside of the individual, is translated and interpreted for us by someone else, and obedience is required to benefit from it.

In contrast, esoteric religion or philosophy is what we call '*Gnostic*', the Greek term for '*Higher Knowledge*' , which is an understanding above and beyond reason.

So, we have these two diverse fundamental positions of teaching and understanding: the literal, religious-and-scientific, on-the-surface of the exoteric position, which requires no transformation of consciousness and is, therefore, accessible to everyone through the sensory mechanism of their five physical senses; and the esoteric position, which goes beyond the five physical senses, to an inner sensing, an inner knowing, an inner mysticism accessed only through a raise in consciousness.

Now, one could be forgiven for thinking that the exoteric literal, scientific position, which requires no transformation in consciousness is the most common and the easier to attain. But, this is not the case! It is the esoteric, mystical, spiritual position which is easier to attain for the average person, if at all spiritually inclined. This mystical, spiritual position which is achieved in meditation, in solitude and quiet in nature. This mystical, spiritual position which transcends the limiting five physical senses. This mystical, spiritual position which gives us access to worlds beyond our physical planet earth, opening for us the doors to the higher celestial energies which surround us on all sides and are constantly waiting to connect with us on a higher energy vibrational level than our mere five physical senses can facilitate. This mystical, spiritual position, this path that cannot be understood from an intellectual level, but only from entering deeply and experiencing it from within.

And it is this esoteric attainment which is rapidly on the increase in these present times, and which differentiates these present times from 2,000 years ago when Jesus walked through the towns and villages of Galilee, teaching and preaching to those who would listen. The conditions under which Jesus worked 2,000 years ago were very different from today. Human consciousness was at a lower state in Jesus' day, with the energies of planet earth being much more dense than they are today. With Jesus, there was the ending of a cycle and the beginning of the cycle of the Age of Pisces. Now the cycle of the Age of Pisces has ended and we are in the new cycle of the Age of Aquarius. Jesus had to adapt his teachings to suit the consciousness of his time, which meant mostly teaching the outer, the exoteric, whereas in these present times we are much more open to the inner, the esoteric.

These present times which we sometimes call the *New Age,* where we are much more open to forms of holistic healing, homeopathy, eastern teachings and practices, and where we access our '*inner',* our meditative or spiritual state.

The *New Age*, where authority comes from our own intuition or higher inspiration, our Higher Self, rather than from the Bible or religious dogmas and teachings, as was the case in the early first century church.

The *New Age*, where we draw from many diverse teachings and beliefs, rather than from the narrow, single external stimulus of the Bible as in Jesus' time.

The *New Age*, where we realise and accept our divine nature, who and what we are as part of the Great Universal God Essence, rather than paying homage to an external, judgemental, punishing God, a male figure somewhere up beyond the clouds, requiring appeasement through constant sacrificial blood offerings, as in the time of Jesus.

The *New Age*, where we realise and accept that the answer to every question we could ever ask is inside ourselves, where we realise that the kingdom of heaven is within ourselves, and where we take responsibility for our own karma, rather than looking to an outside source of authority for forgiveness of our sins and an outside source of authority to set the rules for us, as in Jesus' time.

The New Age, where we realise that we are all one in the Great Universal God Energy, where I am you and you are me, where the *'I',* the '*Me'* and the '*Mine'* have been transformed into the '*Us*', the '*We*' and the '*Ours*'.

The *New Age,* where we see each other as sparks of Divine Light, Divine Essence, and because we acknowledge this Divinity in each other, and in each and every other form of life, we do not criticise, we do not judge, we do not condemn and we certainly do not harm or kill any other form of life.

The *New Age,* where we know that the universe is a loving universe, constantly supporting us and providing our every need.

The Jesus of this *New Age* is much more profound and more accessible than the Jesus of orthodox Christianity. Orthodox Christianity which teaches us that Jesus was born a god, so far removed from all of us that we will never get to where he is. The Jesus of the *New Age*, in comparison, teaches us that we will get to where he is, he reincarnated just like us, and had to follow the laws of this dense world of matter, just like us. He was not all-knowing when he was born, and just like us, he had to leave that behind at his soul level, and learn all over again the process of integrating with God while here on earth. We must all learn again, in our new body, what our soul has always known, that which is locked in the veiled memory banks of our own being. We must all manifest our own Christ perfection, and it was Jesus who showed us the way.

So, when we remember the chapter on the Temple and how

Jewish life 2,000 years ago centered around the flamboyant ceremonies and sacrificial offerings constantly going on there, and compare the limiting, biased, blinkered beliefs and customs of those first-century Jewish people to ourselves in this *New Age,* then we can easily see how and why Jesus made so many enemies when he was in this world.

Jesus repeatedly rebuked the religious authorities of his day, incurring their wrath. Those authorities who set themselves up as the one and only gate-way between human beings and God. Those authorities who created a belief system that no human being could get to God without first going through orthodox religion and its hierarchy of self-appointed ministers. Those authorities who declared that only belief in the outer doctrines, the dogmas, the church teachings, could save a person.

And of course, who made up those doctrines? Those very same authorities! It certainly wasn't Jesus!

It was this closed mindedness, this controlling power structure, with all its limiting teachings and dogmas that Jesus came to destroy, and to rid people of the false teachings which were put in place, not by God, but in God's name, in order to exert control. Jesus' message was completely eclipsed and distorted, making Jesus himself into an idol, so far removed above man that we would never be able to imitate him or get to where he is in the spiritual hierarchy. Even worse, those of us who ever thought we were like Jesus or could be like him, were guilty of heresy and blasphemy. And we all know only too well how the church down through the last 2,000 years has dealt with heretics and blasphemers!

Jesus knew full well what he was doing:

"Do not think that I have come to bring peace to the world. No, I did not come to bring peace, but a sword. I came to set sons against their fathers, daughters against their mothers, daughters-in-law against their mothers-in-law, your worst enemies will be the members of your own family." (Matthew 11:34-36)

So what is this sword about which Jesus speaks?

It is the sword of truth, the sword that will sever and decimate the veils of illusion that surround us. The sword that will cut us free from the shackles and chains of onerous, oppressive, burdening religions. The sword that will separate the untruths and the distortions from the truth. The sword that will cleave the unreal from the real.

"*I came to set the world on fire, and how I wish it were already kindled. I have a baptism to receive, and how distressed I am until it is over. Do you suppose that I came to bring peace to the world? No, not peace, but division. From now on a family of five will be divided, three against two and two against three. Fathers will be against their sons, and sons against their fathers, mothers will be against their daughters, and daughters against their mothers; mothers-in-law will be against their daughters-in-law, and daughters-in-law against their mothers-in-law."* (Luke 13: 49-53)

Speaking to his disciples, Jesus said:

"The world cannot hate you, but it hates me, because I keep telling it that its ways are bad." (John 7:9)

Jesus, in his criticism of "*this godless and wicked day*", (Mark 8:38), in his outspoken championing of the poor, the lower classes, sinners and women, in teaching people to stop worshiping idols and end blood sacrifices to appease an angry god, and in challenging the false priests who subjugated and controlled the people, was sending loud and clear messages to the priests and ruling classes, messages which they did not want to hear, and for which they threatened his life. He made it quite clear to everyone that "*this godless and wicked day*" was not the right way to live and had to end.

"After this, Jesus travelled in Galilee; he did not want to travel in Judea, because the Jewish authorities there were wanting to kill him". (John 7:1)

Even when he was dying on the cross:

"*The chief priests and the teachers of the Law and the elders jeered at him.*" (Matthew 27:41)

And why did they jeer at him?

Because he had claimed "*The Father and I are one.*" Blasphemy, to them!

But Jesus was simply claiming his divine identity, his divine origins, his divine essence. And he had tried to teach them to claim their divine nature as well. But they did not understand. To them this was blasphemy! No man could be like God!

They could not understand that Jesus was teaching that we are all individualised versions of the totality of God.

And not just the priests and ruling classes, but also ordinary Jewish people, who did not understand the esoteric meaning of Jesus' words, and felt their way of life threatened by him:

"Then they picked up stones to throw at him, but Jesus hid himself and left the Temple." (John 8: 58)

" *'The Father and I are one.' Then the people again picked up stones to throw at him."* (John 10:30)

"There was much whispering about him in the crowd. 'He is a good man', some people said. 'No', others said, 'he is misleading the people.' But no one talked about him openly, because they were afraid of the Jewish authorities." (John 7:12-13)

And even more sinister:

"When the people in the synagogue heard this, they were filled with anger. They rose up, dragged Jesus out of the town, and took him to the top of the hill on which their town was built. They meant to throw him over the cliff, but he walked through the middle of the crowd and went his way." (Luke 4:28-30)

Jesus spelt the danger out clearly to his disciples:

"After this the Lord chose another 72 men and sent them out two by two, to go ahead of him to every town and place where he himself was about to go. He said to them, 'There is a large harvest, but few workers to gather it in. Go! I am sending you like lambs among wolves'. " (Luke 10:1-3)

Maybe now we can see why the first century Jewish historian Josephus neglected to include much about Jesus in his prolific writings! Probably because he, like many others, looked upon Jesus as a mere agitator, a trouble maker, a blasphemer and a dedicated destroyer of their religion!

Pre-packaged religion was more acceptable to them. It suited them, as it does many people today, to hand over responsibility to an external force who make the laws and promise us if we obey these laws, then we will get to heaven. How easy is that! How utterly convenient! How liberating from responsibility! Hand everything over to them and we just tag along! No involvement required!

But that is not liberating! It is the direct opposite! Organised, orthodox, pre-packaged religion confines us, curtails us, suffocates us under a plethora of dogmas, doctrines and laws. How can that be liberating? Organised, pre-packaged religion prevents our soul from flying freely, singing its own rapturous, glorious, joyful song, as it is meant to do, free from the shackles and chains, luxuriating in its own unlimited potentiality as divine essence, as an individualised, unique expression of the totality, the wholeness of God!

Now that's what is meant by liberating!

So we need to take heed of Leonardo da Vinci's words:

"The natural desire of good men is knowledge."

Jesus taught an inner, mystical path whereby we attain a higher state of consciousness, and it is this higher state of consciousness that is the true kingdom of heaven. The dominant Christian churches, however, have created a belief system of salvation which is in complete contrast to Jesus' teachings, being based on outward expressions of faith and piety. All through history, mankind has been searching for the key to happiness and contentment. But without success! And why? Simply because mankind has been constantly, time and time again, looking in all the wrong places! That's why the result has always been the same! Complete failure! The only way to achieve happiness and contentment is to go within, and bring about a radical change in one's own consciousness, in one's own spiritual awareness.

And so Jesus incurred the wrath of the priests of the Temple, the wrath of the Pharisees and the wrath of the Sadducees, the main fractious sects in Jewish society. While they believed in external salvation, later promised also by mainstream Christianity, Jesus taught a mystical, inner path to a higher state of consciousness.

As we have already seen, Jews in first century Palestine had deep religious convictions. They saw their obligation to protect and keep whole the divine doctrines and teachings of their faith. Jesus, to them, was guilty of sedition, treason, not only to their national life, but of treason to the higher and God-given life of the religious government of their race, the chosen ones of God, as they sincerely and zealously believed. Jesus to them appeared an enemy of church and state.

Josephus, in his '*Antiquities of the Jews*' bears testimony to this greatest fear of the Jews, fear of contagion or corruption of their religious beliefs from outside sources:

"But now Pilate, the procurator of Judea, removed the army from Cesarea to Jerusalem, to take their winter quarters there, in order

to abolish the Jewish laws. So he introduced Caesar's effigies, which were upon the ensigns, and brought them into the city; whereas our law forbids us the very making of images; on which account the former procurators were wont to make their entry into the cith with such ensigns as had not those ornaments. Pilate was the first who brought those images to Jerusalem, and set them up there: which was done without the knowledge of the people, because it was done in the night time; but as soon as they knew it, they came in multitudes to Cesarea, and interceded with Pilate many days that he would remove the images; and when he would not grant their requests, because it would tend to the injury of Caesar, while they persevered in their request, on the sixth day he ordered his soldiers to have their weapons privately, while he came and sat upon his judgment-seat, which seat was so prepared in the open place of the city, that it concealed the army that lay ready to oppress them; and when the Jews petitioned him again, he gave a signal to the soldiers to encompass them routed, and threatened that their punishment should be no less than immediate death, unless they would leave off disturbing him, and go their ways home. But they threw themselves upon the ground, and laid their necks bare, and said they would take their death very willingly, rather than the wisdom of their laws should be transgressed; upon which Pilate was deeply affected with their firm resolution to keep their laws inviolable, and presently commanded the images to be carried back from Jerusalem to Cesarea." (*'Antiquities of the Jews'*, Chapter 18, pages 55-59)

So this was how seriously the Jews protected their religious beliefs! And here was Jesus contaminating and corrupting those beliefs!

Even the Roman authorities understood that the demands for the death of Jesus did not arise from personal spite or the satisfaction of any revenge against the individual, but solely because they believed and so declared that Jesus was an enemy, a would-be destroyer of the divine faith and teachings of the Israelite nation and a seducer of the people. And so he had to be got rid of!

And when we look more closely at these teachings of Jesus, at both his exoteric teachings, exemplified by the limited understandings of Peter and most of the other disciples, and the esoteric teachings, those inner, deep meanings, exemplified by the higher understandings of Jesus' spiritual partner and equal, Mary Magdalene, and the disciple John, then we can see that Jesus was a man ahead of his time. Jesus was a man not understood on the spiritual level by most of those who listened to him, those who could see only references to the physical world in his words, believing his kingdom was in this world and he was about to rescue them all from the oppression of the Romans and bring about God's kingdom on earth, when in actual fact he was talking about the spiritual worlds, to which we are all returning when the time is right, to merge again with the Godhead. But none of this they understood. They firmly believed that Jesus was about to lead an armed uprising against Roman oppression and set all the Israelites free. And yes! He was trying to set them free! From the real oppression of the religious authorities who had placed themselves as the only doorway to their God.

So let us take a closer look now at Jesus the Teacher, and find the esoteric, the inner understanding of his words, which his first-century Jewish contemporaries failed to do, and to understand his teachings, which the early Christian Church fathers distorted and manipulated for their own devious mercenary ends, establishing a frightening, judgemental, punishing God, holding people to ransom through lies about a hell of fire for eternity for those who displeased and a seat at the right hand of God for all eternity for those who pleased.

All this nonsense, false teachings and false dogmas from which Jesus came to set us free!

So what exactly was Jesus teaching?

"Jesus preached his messages to the people, using many other parables like these; he told them as much as they could understand. He would not speak to them without using parables, but when he was alone with his disciples, he would explain everything to them." (Mark 4:33-34)

"Then the disciples came to Jesus and asked him, 'Why do you use parables when you talk to the people?'

Jesus answered. 'The knowledge about the secrets of the Kingdom of heaven has been given to you, but not to them. For the person who has something will be given more, so that he will have more than enough; but the person who has nothing will have taken away from him even the little he has. The reason I use parables in talking to them is that they look, but do not see, and they listen, but do not hear.' " (Matthew 13:10-13)

However, even though Jesus made things simple through his parables, even the disciples, with the exceptions of Mary Magdalene and John, appeared to be quite stupid at times and failed to get the meaning!

Jesus was most certainly and purposely, deliberately and intentionally teaching on those two levels, the esoteric and the exoteric.

And why? Because he knew that most people were not yet ready to raise their spiritual consciousness to understand and accept his teachings.

So if Jesus knew all that, then why did he reincarnate in first-century Jewish Palestine?

Jesus was sowing the seed! The seed which would take almost 2,000 years of earth time to sprout and grow!

At this point in time, we are experiencing a great spiritual awakening, a massive raise in spiritual consciousness, enabling us to accept the teachings of Jesus:

"*He that hath ears, let them hear!*"

It is only when we raise our spiritual awareness, our spiritual consciousness, that we can understand! It is only then that we can actually hear what Jesus is trying to tell us! And we can only hear that when we are ready! When we have achieved a high enough spiritual vibration to enable us to hear!

So what were these profound, all-encompassing doctrines which Jesus proclaimed, but which have been so distorted or discarded in favour of man-made notions of salvation, to be supposedly achieved through rites and ceremonies?

There is one message, just one, that is so fundamental and pivotal to all of Jesus' teachings, which, if we understand fully, opens the door to all the other messages, but which, if we fail to understand, hinders us from getting what Jesus was all about in his ministry.

That one profound message which is inter-woven and inter-twined with all his other messages! That one profound message, which, when understood, automatically leads us to an understanding of all the other messages! They all follow in natural progression from that one profound teaching!

So what is this one profound message that opens all the doors?

The Truth Will Set You Free

Jesus said:

"You will know the truth and the truth will set you free". (John 8:32)

These words of Jesus have been quoted down through history for the last 2,000 years. But what do they actually mean?

What is this *truth* about which Jesus is speaking? The *truth* about what?

And how can we be *set free*? More importantly, from what exactly are we to be *set free*?

Does it mean that once we know the truth, whatever that truth may be, then we are free to behave as we like? To do as we wish? To live an unrestrained life of indulging in self-will?

I greatly doubt it!

Or does it mean that when we learn the truth about our own divine nature, we will be free from the shackles and chains of dictatorial and controlling powers?

Is that then, why the truth has been denied us all these years? What is there in the truth that those powers are so fearful of us discovering?

This message '*the truth will set you free*' ties in with other words of Jesus, the words that reveal his most profound, fundamental teaching, the teaching that opens all the other doors to understanding:

"Ye are gods, as I am." (John 10:34)

" 'You are gods', I said; 'all of you are children of the Most High.' " (Psalms 82:6)

And:

"Philip said to him, 'Lord, show us the Father; that is all we need.'

Jesus answered, 'For a long time I have been with you all; yet you do not know me, Philip? Whoever has seen me has seen the Father ....I am in the Father and the Father is in me...........I am telling you the truth: those who believe in me will do what I do - yes, they will do even greater things.' " (John 14:9-12)

There it is!

The core teaching of Jesus!

Yes! The very core teaching of Jesus!

The pivot of all his teachings!

The reason why he was accused and condemned to death for blasphemy!

Yet, to this day, this core teaching of Jesus has been and is being deliberately ignored.

This core teaching of Jesus which is the vital key to our understanding of our own inherent divine nature. This core teaching of Jesus which is the vital key to our raising of our spiritual consciousness. This core teaching of Jesus which is the vital key to our understanding of our own reality. And if we ignore this vital key to our own reality, if we reject our own inner divinity, then we cannot find peace or happiness. And we cannot progress above the dense earth vibrational energy frequency level.

*"Jesus said to them, 'I came to show human possibilities. What has been created by me, all men can create. And that which I am, all men will be.' " (*Ancient Tibetan Manuscript quoted by Russian anthropologist Nicholas Roerich in his 1926 work '*Himalaya*' and by Elizabeth Clare Prophet in her 1997 publication '*Access the Power of Your Higher Self*')

What Jesus was trying to get into their heads was the divinity of all men, not just the divinity of himself. And the divine in all of us means that the power of God, the essential spirit, is within each of us. And being of the divine means we each have unlimited potential.

So the *truth* bit was exactly this: we are all of divine nature, divine essence, God essence, just as Jesus was. And that is why Jesus could say:

'The Father and I are one.' (John 10:30)

'.........even though you do not believe me, you should at least believe my deeds, in order that you may know once and for all that the Father is in me and that I am in the Father.' (John 10:38)

And this was why Jesus was accused of blasphemy and his life threatened. But he was simply acknowledging his God essence and trying to get others to acknowledge the same in themselves. God is not external to us. And if we continue to see God as outside of ourselves, as external to us, then we are seeing our own limitations, instead of the unlimited potentiality of our own divinity.

Likewise, when he said:

"Be perfect as your heavenly Father is perfect." (Matthew 5:48)

Here Jesus was, yet again, referring to the God energy in all of us and our potential for perfection. He was telling us to try and attain the highest of all ideals, that of achieving our own Christ Consciousness which is inherent in all of us.

And when we acknowledge and accept this *truth* in ourselves, that we are of divine nature, that we are spiritual beings having a physical experience, we will be *set free* to be the best we can be, to reach our full, unlimited potential as sparks of divine essence, and not just mere physical bodies. We will be *set free* from the shackles and chains of orthodox religions telling us we are mere mortals, sinners, limited by our five physical senses, destined to hell or heaven for all eternity.

By acknowledging our divinity and the divinity in all persons and the divinity in all forms of life, this is how we raise our spiritual awareness, our spiritual consciousness. This is how we evolve our immortal soul, the very reason why we came here into this incarnation! Raising our consciousness simply means realising and accepting our divine, unlimited potentiality.

Dense physical matter makes people forget or deny that they are spiritual beings. They deny the very existence of God, and therefore they cannot transcend their current level of spiritual consciousness.

So that basic, profound teaching of Jesus, which most people failed to get, was that we are all divine essence, we all share in the divinity of God. God is within each and every one of us. We have total access to that inner divinity at all times. We do not need any middle-men to intercede on our behalf between us and God. The kingdom of God is within. Not in any temple, not in any church, but within each one of us. We do not have to partake in elaborate, flamboyant ceremonies or rituals in order to connect. And we certainly do not need to rhyme off learned and repeated prayers or platitudes, glibly recited, in order to connect with God. We are God essence already! It's all within ourselves! We need look no further than inside ourselves!

So we can clearly see why the powers who set themselves up as being in control of our soul evolution are so fearful of us finding out the truth about what Jesus really taught! As we find the truth out more and more, those same powers become defunct, redundant, irrelevant, extinct! They are struggling for their very survival! They are desperately struggling, though against all the odds, to retain control and power!

You are Gods, even as I am

Now let me explain this '*you are God*' more clearly, as Jesus specified several times.

Language is a very limiting medium when trying to get across spiritual teachings. Human words cannot do full justice to the meaning of what Jesus taught, or to spiritual concepts.

Believing that each of us is God is not some sort of spiritual arrogance or blasphemy. You are of God essence, a part of, not apart from, your divine origins, your divine source. You are an individualised identity, inherent in the whole concept that is the Universal God Energy. You are an expression of God's creativity, and as such you are unique in yourself, but you are not ALL that God is. You are part of the whole, but you are NOT the whole. God has a universal sense of identity, and you have a personalised sense of identity within that universal identity. You are a personalised, unique expression of God, within the vastness of the totality of God, co-creating with God within that vastness. God is the totality. Each of us is an individualised, a unique and precious part within that totality.

WOW! Is this not mind-blowing?

Think of it like this! The wave is contained in the sea. Outside of the sea, the wave can have no existence. The wave is only there because the sea is there. But within that sea, the wave has its own identity, its own form of expression, created or thrown up by the sea, which is its source. So if there is no sea, then there can be no wave. When the wave breaks, it changes form, it is no longer a wave, but it is still contained in the sea. As a wave, it is just one expression of the sea, unique from all the other waves, one individualised element of the sea, but it is not the entire ocean. And whether it is a wave or has ceased being a wave for the moment, it always remains the same essence as the sea, in this case, water.

So think of God as the entire ocean, and each of us as a wave in that ocean, each of us an individualised expression of the totality of God.

When you drop your finger into the ocean and then hold it up, you see a tiny sparkling drop of water. All the elements, all the qualities of the ocean are in that tiny droplet. That tiny droplet is an individualised part of the ocean. In the very same way, all the elements of God are found within each one of us. We are each a drop of water from the vast ocean. We all have the qualities of the whole ocean, of infinite reality, but not the quantity of the whole ocean. And just as the droplet of water in the ocean merges back again into the whole ocean, we too will only be all that we are supposed to be when we merge back into our Real Self, our Christ Self, God. It is our self-instilled, or religion-instilled sense of separation from God that keeps us from the reality of ourselves.

And this is what Jesus tried to teach his disciples. We are all individualised expressions of the creativity of God, and as such, each of us is God in that we are that individualised expression, but we are not God in the entirety of what God is. We are not ALL that God is. But we are definitely a part of what God is. God is NOT external to us. There is a divine dimension within all persons.

See how this all differs so greatly from what orthodox religions have been teaching?

They have been teaching that God is an external male force outside of ourselves, someone to whom we pray for forgiveness for our sins, for we are definitely sinners. That God is a severe, judgemental, punishing God, remotely positioned somewhere high up beyond the clouds. And Jesus was '*his only begotten son'*, that one person who shared God's divinity.

See the difference from Jesus' teaching that we are all of divine nature, just like him? Jesus taught us that we all share the same divine origin.

Now let us take this a step further. If you are an individualised element within the totality of God, and hence you have unlimited potential, then every time you think "*I can't do this*" or "*That is way beyond me*" or "*I could never achieve that*", then what are you actually doing?

What you are actually doing, every and each time you limit yourself in any way, is denying the power of God, proclaiming the limitations of God! But God is totally unlimited!

And there is more to consider! As an individualised version of God, and at the same time all in the entire consciousness of God, all united in the Great Universal Consciousness of God, that makes us all One. I am you and you are me. So how can I hate or kill you, if by doing so, I am hating or killing myself? How can I hate or hurt any form of life, if I AM that form of life?

And that explains the following words of Jesus:

"Then Jesus' mother and brothers arrived. They stood outside the house and sent in a message, asking for him. A crowd was sitting round Jesus, and they said to him, 'Look, your mother and your brothers and sisters are outside and they want you.'

Jesus answered, 'Who is my mother? Who are my brothers?' He looked at the people sitting round him and said, 'Look! Here are my mother and my brothers! Whosoever does what God wants him to do is my brother, my sister, my mother.' " (Mark: 3:31-35)

So the divinity within each of us was the core teaching of Jesus. But it was blasphemy to the first century Jewish people who really believed in a punishing, admonishing God who needed to be appeased by blood sacrifices.

And it was these teachings of Jesus, contrary to all Jewish beliefs, that resulted in him being so hated by the Jewish authorities:

"' 'We do not want to stone you because of any good deeds, but because of your blasphemy! You are only a man, but you are trying to make yourself God!'

Jesus answered, 'It is written in your own Law that God said, 'You are gods. God called those people gods, the people to whom his message was given.' " (John 10:34)

Jesus was repeating the words of the Old Testament:

" 'You are gods,' I said; 'All of you are children of the Most High.' " (Psalm 82:6)

And "*setting us free*" ? What did Jesus mean by this?

Jesus meant bringing us spiritual freedom, wisdom and the realisation that there is much more to life than the physical and the material. The material world is just a facade, hiding the underlying spiritual reality. But Jesus' contemporaries failed to understand. Their consciousness was not yet at a high enough level to take all of this in. They believed Jesus was about to free them from the oppression of Roman rule, and that was imminent! Any moment now, God would appear in the clouds with his army of angels and bring them freedom. And with that in their minds, everything Jesus said they interpreted as just what they wanted to hear.

Energy and how it works

Before we consider the next teachings of Jesus and before we can fully understand any of them, we need to understand energy and the numerous and countless energy vibrational frequency levels that permeate the entire cosmos.

Everything, absolutely everything in existence and that ever has been in existence is energy. Energy, as vibration, is constantly changing, taking different forms, and operating on different frequency levels, from the highest right down to the lowest level. Planet earth here is the most dense form of energy, the world of form and solid matter, the level at which most soul learning is available, hence the reason why souls want to reincarnate time and time again, in order to evolve our spiritual consciousness, to increase our spiritual and soul awareness and the spiritual consciousness of all humanity. While we are physically embodied here on this earth plane, our five physical senses, activated fully at birth, are the instruments that are designed to detect the vibrations all around us in this material world, the world of matter, the world of form, the world around us which we perceive with our human eyes.

But we also have inner sensory mechanisms, our chakras, which are designed to detect vibrations that are beyond the material world. These are our inner senses, which allow us to detect the vibrations of spiritual energy frequency levels and spiritual light.

The only difference between what we can visibly see with our human eyes and the invisible things beyond our human vision is a difference in energy vibration. The only difference between our material universe and the higher levels of the spirit worlds is a difference in energy vibration. So the only difference between our earth and what we call heaven is a difference in vibration. Only a thin veil of energy separates our material world from the spiritual world. The higher up through the energy levels you progress, the lighter, the higher your energy becomes, the faster your energy vibrates.

And yes, there is a dividing line, a barrier between all the various energy levels, right up through the spiritual hierarchy. But it is by no means an impenetrable barrier. You are meant to cross all those barriers. Your consciousness has the ability, even while here on the earth plane, to cross those barriers between the material world and the spiritual world, and countless people have done so and are continuing to do so. But in order to do so, it takes a shift in your consciousness. Your physical senses and your lower earth consciousness level can never access even the lowest level of the spiritual universe. But your consciousness is just like a dial on a radio. You can tune into other higher frequencies, but you need to know how to manage the dial. In order to control the dial, you first need to accept that God does indeed exist. Then you need to understand that you are not just a physical body, but more importantly, you are a spiritual body having a physical experience for a short time only. Then you need to rid yourself of any notion of any separation between you and God. This all raises your spiritual consciousness, and raising your spiritual consciousness is a pre-requisite for tuning into higher energy frequency levels. And tuning into other higher level frequencies is what feeds and nourishes your soul, your immortal spiritual body.

As we increase our spiritual awareness, our spiritual soul awareness, through learning the lessons we came here to earth to learn, we progress up through the ranks, up through the hierarchy of the energy frequency levels in the spirit world, continuing to learn at soul level, continuing to progress, and attaining the various levels to which our learning successes have given us access. We cannot progress any further than the particular level to which we have earned access. In other words, we can only access the levels as we earn the right to do so. Higher levels can always descend to lower levels in order to facilitate a meeting with loved ones, but lower level energy souls cannot ascend to higher levels until they earn that right to do so.

So, contrary to general belief, the spirit world itself is not a static place of existence. There is constant upwards movement through the countless vibrational energy levels that all make up the celestial kingdoms, and, as we have just seen, we can only access each one of those in turn when we have earned the right to entry, by the ongoing evolutionary process of our soul journey.

Jesus came from the highest vibrational frequency, the energy level nearest the Godhead. Look at it like an onion. The centre is the heart of the onion, the strongest part, and the layers going outwards get less potent as they go further from the centre.

We are now ready to consider the next of Jesus' teachings:

" *I have yet many things to say to you, but ye cannot bear them now.*" (John 18:12)"

And:

'I shall not be with you very much longer. You will look for me; but I tell you now what I told the Jewish authorities, you cannot go where I am going...............'

'Where are you going, Lord?' Simon Peter asked him.

'You cannot follow me now where I am going', answered Jesus, 'but

later you will follow me.' (John 13:33-35)

So, once we understand the concept of energy and how it all works, we can easily understand what Jesus was trying to explain to his disciples here. But they could not understand what he meant when he said they could not go where he was going. They could not go where he was going simply because they had not evolved spiritually to that level. But in time they would!

This puts into context Jesus' words, repeated constantly throughout the gospels:

"Listen, then, if you have ears!' (Matthew 13:9)

This was not some sort of sarcastic or admonishing comment! Of course we all have ears! But we all do not hear! And that's because we are not yet ready to hear! We have not yet raised our energy frequency level to that level which enables us to hear!

But Jesus was speaking to those who were ready to listen, those who were on a high enough spiritual energy vibrational level to take in what he was saying. Those who were able to cross the divide between the dense energy of the material world and the higher energy frequency levels of the spirit world.

I Am The Light Of The World

Now let us consider these words of Jesus:

"*Jesus spoke to the Pharisees again. 'I am the light of the world', he said. 'Whoever follows me will have the light of life and will never walk in darkness.'* " (John 8:12-13)

And:

"Thomas said to him, 'Lord, we do not know where you are going, so how can we know the way to get there?'

Jesus answered him, 'I am the way, the truth and the life; no one goes to the Father except by me.' " (John 14: 5-6)

And:

"*I am come that all might have life and that they might have it more abundantly*". (John 10:10)

Now, if we understand the previous teachings, these words are easy to understand!

Jesus was saying that it is only by accepting our own divinity that we can understand the nature of God, and only by accepting our own divinity can we progress up through the hierarchal ranks of the spirit world to attain full spiritual awareness and re-merge with the Godhead. If we do not listen to the words of Jesus and accept his messages, then we will remain in the lower dense energy levels of matter, unable to progress further up the spiritual ranks.

We are all of the same divine potential as Jesus. The only difference is that Jesus has already, a long time ago, realised his full divine potential. And because we are of divine essence and divine unlimited potential, each and every person is innately good. Each one of us is a potential Christ, but few of us realise it! The perfection of the Christ Consciousness within is the aim of all of us. Jesus demonstrated to us that we can achieve this spiritual perfection, this Christ Consciousness, just as he has.

Hence Jesus' words:

"*Be ye therefore perfect as your Father in heaven is perfect.*" (Matthew 5:48)

We are all destined for perfection, for full Christ Consciousness, which is the highest energy vibrational frequency within the entire God Energy.

Jesus is the master-teacher, the guide who came to guide us back to our true nature, the guide who knows the road because he has travelled it before us and has levelled it out for us. But he cannot carry us along that road. We have to walk it ourselves, following him. And if we follow him, he will lead us to the truth of who and what we really are, and thereby gain access to the higher spiritual levels. Jesus will not lead us to material things of this world, because that is not what our existence is all about. We are here on this earth plane not to accumulate vast material riches or possessions, but to evolve our immortal souls. Yes, we are living here on planet earth, we need material possessions in order to survive, but we do not need to get immersed in them. Our physical body is only an outer garment, a vehicle to transport our immortal soul through this life-time, a clothing which we will discard when we no longer need it.

"But he answered and said, 'It is written, Man shall not live by bread alone, but by every word that proceedeth out of the mouth of God.' " (Matthew 4:4)

"And Jesus answered him, saying, 'It is written, that man shall not live by bread alone, but by every word of God.' " (Luke 4:4)

Bread is symbolic of food to nourish the physical body. But man is a spiritual being, first and foremost, and that aspect of him must also be nourished. And that aspect can only be nourished by a raising of consciousness, by an awareness of, and an accepting of our divine potential. It is absolutely imperative that in order to raise our spiritual consciousness, we need to drop any sense of duality or ego and accept that we are one with divinity. There can be no separation.

Jesus went further than this.

Performing good deeds, doing charitable acts, donating to charity, living a peaceful life, forgiving people who offend or hurt you, living an honest life, teaching your children right from wrong, praying, attending religious services, - all of this is good and worthy, yes, but it is not enough! All of this simply makes you a *good person.* It does NOT push you further up the cosmic spiritual elevator to a higher spiritual vibrational frequency!

So we can clearly see the meaning of the following:

"*Flesh and blood cannot enter the kingdom of heaven.*" (Corinthians 15:50))

This means that it takes you to be much more than just a *good person* in order to attain Spiritual Awareness. You cannot advance any further up the spiritual ladder until you raise your spiritual consciousness. You simply cannot advance up through the spiritual hierarchy if you are still in your dense consciousness, the dense consciousness of life on planet earth, the dense consciousness that keeps you in the mind-set that you are only a physical being. You must rid yourself of the lower mind consciousness before you can access the spiritual higher vibrations.

When you pass over to the next dimension after your earthly sojourn here as an embodied spirit, you cannot claim that because you have been a *good person* you are therefore entitled to a spiritual reward, a foot further up the spiritual ladder. You can only proceed upwards through the spiritual vibrations if you have achieved the required levels of spiritual awareness required for each level. Only if you have successfully managed to raise your spiritual consciousness. Your soul does not gravitate towards any particular level determined by the amount of good deeds you have done. The spiritual levels are not demarcated or differentiated by the number of good deeds done or the amount of money given to charity. The spiritual levels are demarcated by the various and countless degrees of consciousness, and whatever level of consciousness your soul is at, whatever level of consciousness your soul has attained at the point of entry into the spirit world, that, and that alone, determines where your soul will gravitate towards. So your primary concern in this earthly incarnation is to raise your spiritual consciousness.

And how is that done? How do you raise your spiritual consciousness?

By acknowledging that you are NOT separate from God! By accepting your divine essence! By seeing yourself, and every other form of life as the divine spiritual light we all really are, and by showing unconditional love for all and sundry! It is what is in your heart that matters, and what is in your heart cannot be hidden from or in the spirit world. Performing charitable acts, donating money to charity, being kind to people, attending church services, praying, just because you feel you must do so, that all this is required in order to enter heaven, then that is not going to achieve for you the result you are hoping for!

Jesus told us:

"When you pray, do not be like the hypocrites, for they love to pray standing in the synagogues and on the street corners to be seen by men. I tell you the truth, they have received their reward in full. But when you pray, go into your room, close the door and pray to your Father, who is unseen. Then your Father, who sees what is done in secret, will reward you. And when you pray, do not keep on babbling like pagans, for they think they will be heard because of their many words. Do not be like them, for your Father knows what you need before you ask him." (Matthew 6:5-15)

So, if you are given to living what you think to be a good life, obeying all the rules, with exemplary behaviour, simply for the reason that you reckon this will all get you into heaven, then, alas and alack, you really are on the wrong track!

Or if you are doing something only for some sort of reward, then again, you are on the wrong track!

Take the disciple Peter:

"Then Peter spoke up. 'Look,' he said, 'we have left everything and followed you. What shall we have?'

Jesus said to them, 'You can be sure that when the Son of Man sits on his glorious throne in the New Age, then you twelve followers of mine will also sit on thrones, to rule the twelve tribes of Israel. And everyone who has left houses or brothers or sisters or father or mother or children or fields for my sake, will receive a hundred times more and will be given eternal life. But many who now are first will be last, and many who now are last will be first.' " (Matthew 19: 27-30)

Peter was stuck in the lower ego vibrations! He was still following Jesus for a self-centered motive, based on the belief that because he has given up something, then he is entitled to a reward or compensation for doing so.

What Peter was actually thinking here was that he had to give up part of his own separate self in order to follow Jesus, and he was willing to do that. But at the same time he was seeking a reward for none other than that same separate self! So, in other words, he was confirming the reality of that separate self! So he was severely limited in how far he could go spiritually, because there is no room for separate self in the process of raising your spiritual consciousness. Dropping your separate self, your ego, is an intrinsic part of the whole process of attaining awareness.

So, we must rid ourselves of the idea that we are doing good deeds, living what we consider a good life, in order to get to heaven and receive a reward there. That's elevating the separate self, and separate self keeps you firmly stuck in the dense consciousness of planet earth. This is what we all need to overcome in order to progress up the spiritual ladder. In fact, it is the first stage in our spiritual evolution. It is the first requisite, the first challenge to be overcome. Get rid of the ego!

This desire for self-gratification comes from the ego. And the ego must be dropped in all its various forms. But the ego is sometimes very difficult to recognise!

Let us look at Peter again:

" 'Where are you going, Lord?' Simon Peter asked him.

'You cannot follow me now where I am going.' answered Jesus, 'but later you will follow me.'

'Lord, why can't I follow you now?' asked Peter. 'I am ready to die for you!'

Jesus answered, 'Are you ready to die for me? I am telling you the truth: before the cock crows you will say three times that you do not know me.' " (John 13: 36-38)

And that was exactly what Peter did! Again, we see a Peter who is still stuck, a Peter who still sees himself as separate from Jesus. Otherwise, if he saw himself as being at Oneness with Jesus, he would not have denied him!

Get the message?

The message is loud and clear!

In order to raise one's own spiritual consciousness, one must abandon completely and forever the notion of doing good works to achieve a reward; the notion of being any better than anyone else because of those good works; the notion that one's good works will save humanity or the planet and will therefore be recognised in the higher spiritual echelons; the notion that one's importance and standing in society will increase as a result of one's good works; the notion that one's powers will increase as a result of one's good works; the notion that one can somehow convert others to a particular creed or belief system by one's good works.

Or if you lead a good life because you fear eternal damnation in hell, then you are also on the wrong track!

You need to raise your spiritual consciousness! And that and that only is what earns you your passage up through the spiritual ranks! Right up to the highest vibration, that of the Christ Consciousness.

When you arrive at the metaphorical pearly gates, the main criteria is not what good deeds you did or how much money you gave to charity! BUT! What level of spiritual consciousness have you attained?

AND! How did you use the energy that was allotted to you out of the great Universal Energy of God?

Man is NOT a body. He HAS a body. But he IS a soul. And we will no longer need this outer garment which we HAVE, to be a vehicle for what we ARE, when we pass back to spirit, taking with us only the brownie points which we have earned in this life-time, those brownie points which are our passport to the higher levels in the spirit world. And those brownie points signify a raise in our spiritual consciousness.

"What shall it profit a man if he gains the whole world, and forfeits

his life?" (Matthew 16:26)

When Jesus walked this earth 2,000 years ago, he had very few followers and was only known in his localised area.

So too, if you yourself are intent on doing good works, that intention must not be veiled, masked or disguised behind the artificial facade of looking for reward, honour or glory. You must be coming from your heart, from genuine unconditional love, with no alternative motives or agenda other than to help that particular person at that particular time, for their own highest good, and not yours. When you are coming from the heart centre energy, everything is effortless.

Likewise, if you are a holistic, Reiki or alternative medicine therapist or practitioner, you must not see yourself as the healer. You are not the healer. You are merely the conduit, the channeller, through which the energy flows from Source.

And if you are a Spiritual teacher or writer, then the same applies. Your intention must be that those whom you are teaching, those who are reading your books, do not see you, but the message you are delivering. You are only the messenger!

So now let us look at and interpret the next message!

WHOEVER SAVES HIS LIFE SHALL LOSE IT AND WHOEVER LOSES HIS LIFE SHALL SAVE IT

"For whosoever will save his life shall lose it: and whosoever will lose his life for my sake shall find it." (Matthew 16:25)

This all sounds very paradoxical!

So what does it mean?

It simply reinforces the previous message that we must lose all desire for self-gratification, we must drop the ego, we must let go of our individual small, human, limited identity and adopt a far greater individual identity within the vastness, within the infinity of the greater identity that is the consciousness of the Universal God energy. We must lose our own individual limited consciousness within the greater consciousness, thereby not losing, but actually gaining a vastly greater consciousness. We as human beings are living on this earth plane, which has not yet ascended, so we adopt a duality, an identity with the body and an identity with the spiritual side of us. In doing this, we see ourself as a separate being, separate from our spiritual self. It is this separate sense of the "it" of the physical body which we need to drop, in order to find the "it" of the spiritual being which we really are. And then and only then, when we find the "it" of the spiritual being can we find the "it" of our true spiritual identity. Only then can we become whole, instead of being divided into two separate identities.

So, coming into oneness with our own spiritual identity means coming into oneness with the God energy. And coming into oneness with the God energy does not mean losing our individual identity. Not at all! It is the direct opposite! We find greater, in fact unlimited scope to expand in our spiritual identity, we find spiritual freedom in our Christhood, unlike when in our separate identity, where we are limited and curtailed by the human ego.

Jesus is telling us that we are letting go of a lesser identity in order to take on a far greater identity. Those of us who are willing to lose the mortal sense of identity, our life, in order to attain the Christ Consciousness identity, then we shall find eternal life through that much greater identity of the Christ Consciousness, rather than this short, temporary life-span here on earth.

"Jesus said (to Pilate), 'My kingdom does not belong to this world; if my kingdom belonged to this world, my followers would fight hard to keep me from being handed over to the Jewish authorities. No, my kingdom does not belong here!'

So Pilate asked him, 'Are you a king then?'

Jesus answered, 'You say that I am a king. I was born and came into the world for this one purpose, to speak about the truth. Whoever belongs to the truth listens to me.' " (John 19: 36-37)

Jesus was bringing us the truth about our very nature. We are spiritual beings, experiencing a physical embodiment yet again, to try and attain the higher levels of existence in the spiritual frequencies. And if we want to achieve complete spiritual evolution, as we all do, then we must start the process of our own ascension, raising our own spiritual consciousness, increasing our own spiritual awareness. Jesus is telling us how we can do this! If we listen to his messages, he is leading us towards that achievement. He is leading us upwards on the ladder of ascension. And not just that! He is holding the ladder as we climb, to steady it for us!

Jesus told us:

"Come to me, all of you who are tired from carrying heavy loads,

and I will give you rest. Take my yoke and put it on you, and learn from me, because I am gentle and humble in spirit; and you will find rest. For the yoke I will give you is easy, and the load I will put on you is light." (Matthew 11:28-30)

How easy it now is to understand it all!

Jesus has already got to where we are going, so he is now helping us along the same path which he has already trod. We make the road hard because we are carrying too many burdens of a physical, material nature, we are too caught up in the heavy, back-breaking weight of the materialism of this physical world. We have separated our spiritual identity from our physical identity. That is what is making our burden heavy, slowing us down. But Jesus is showing us how to move faster along the road by lightening our burden.

It could not possibly be any more simple!

But Jesus' disciples, apart from Mary Magdalene and John the Beloved, could not understand because they were not spiritually developed enough to understand. But now, 2,000 years later, we have a much greater understanding of Jesus' words. Jesus sowed the seed, and that seed is now sprouting and growing.

And talking about sowing seeds, it is now time for us to consider the following words of Jesus:

"*You have a saying: 'Four more months and then the harvest.' But I tell you, take a good look at the field; the crops are now ripe and ready to be harvested."* (John 4:35)

The grain is already involved in the seed. Anything that can be, already is! Whatever you ask for is already out there!

Just think for a moment about the wonder of that statement! The power we have to manifest whatever it is we want!

But! And there is always a but with humans! We are limiting ourselves by remaining in our dense, material, physical consciousness. Physical matter is so dense that we can so easily lose sight of our divine origins, and so begins the downward spiral. We cannot transcend this dense consciousness until we accept that we are first and foremost spiritual, much more than we are physical.

Then the limitations that we have set upon ourselves will vanish! Then the door to the wonders of the universe will open to us! Then we will live life as we know, deep down in our own being, we are meant to live it!

Bring it on!

The Law of Abundance

It is not a sin to be rich!

We live in a rich and abundant universe!

A rich and abundant universe where everything flows in a natural, dance-like, magnetic, synchronised movement to exactly where it is wanted and needed! And we just need to go with the flow!

Richness and abundance is our natural state of being!

And Jesus illustrated this to us!

Where? In the miracle of the loaves and fishes! And again in the miracle of the fishing nets being filled to bursting!

Yes, those two miracles in particular, illustrate the law of abundance!

Jesus was not a magician with a magic wand, uttering such magic words as "*Abrakadabra*" or "*Kalimazoo*"! And hey presto! All this stuff comes out of the blue!

But that is the image we have been presented with by orthodox religion!

Let us take a look at the prime example, the so-called miracle of the loaves and fishes.

A miracle?

It was not in actual fact a miracle at all, in the sense that we perceive a miracle to be some supernatural happening or the result of some supernatural intervention.

Jesus was NOT some sort of weird magician, waving his magic wand about. He was operating completely and totally within the natural law, the law of natural abundance! And that is the law that the parable of the loaves and fishes was created to illustrate!

So simple when you understand it all!

The loaves and fishes were already out there! Jesus just drew the extra food to him! He understood totally the law of abundance, the natural laws of the universe and the natural laws of the cosmos.

Now I was not there, nor do I know anyone else who was there! So I can only speculate as to how the extra food actually materialised!

Nor do I know for certain that this actually happened! Remember! A lot of the gospel stories were created to illustrate certain teachings.

One thing I do know for certain though, is that loaves and fishes did not suddenly start to fall out of the sky on top of the crowd after Jesus performed some magic trick! Perhaps a passing caravan of camels, laden with food on its way to somewhere or other provided the food. Perhaps someone from Jerusalem got it out there. Or perhaps some of the people themselves had food with them, so much so that when they all shared it out, they had so much left over that twelve baskets were filled! Who knows?

Abundance! That was the lesson! The food was already out there! All Jesus needed to do was image it and call it forth into manifestation. No "*Abrakadabra!*" No "*Kalimazoo!*" No magic words or magic wands waving about! No need for any of that! Just an understanding of the natural, unfailing law of natural abundance. And Jesus had full and complete knowledge and understanding of that law at the highest level. There was no shred of doubt in his mind! And that was because Jesus had raised his consciousness far beyond the mortal, material, dense, limited earth consciousness.

The same with the so-called miracle of the fishing nets being filled to bursting after Peter and some of the other disciples had been out all night fishing and had caught nothing. Nothing? Not even one little fish? And after being out fishing all night?

The fish that materialised were not just suddenly created out of nothing. Nor did they suddenly fall from the sky, no more than the loaves and fishes did in the previous so-called miracle! Fish falling from the sky? Right into Peter's nets?

No! The fish were already there in the sea! Jesus simply called them to him! Just another example of the law of abundance in operation!

"Ye are Gods! What I do you too can do and more!"

Get the message? Anything we need or want is already out there! Already out there in a world of abundance! All we have to do is image it and call it forth into manifestation!

Look at it this way. You too have often seen money or whatever it is you have desired just appear out of what seemed like nowhere! At that moment in time, when you were short of money to buy that food or pay that bill, and you were desperately wondering where you were ever going to get it, suddenly it appeared from what seemed like out of nowhere! But it didn't appear from out of nowhere! Nobody created or printed new money notes for you! It was out there all the time, and you just drew it to you with the energy you sent out to the universe in the form of your thoughts!

"Are ye not Gods, even as I am?" That's what Jesus was telling us. We have the power to draw all things to us! We have the power to satisfy our needs and desires with our own thoughts!

The glass is either half full or half empty. It all depends on your perspective and on your state of consciousness whether you see this universe as a place of want or a place of abundance for all. If you see this universe as a place of scarcity and want, that is exactly what you will get. And likewise, if you see this universe as a place of richness and abundance, that is also what you will get. It is totally up to you as to what you get in life! So instead of seeing what you do not have, just start to think about all that you do have. All that the universe is doing for you and sending to you day after day after day.

So remember! Abundance and lack are both states of consciousness. And according to your state of consciousness, you create your own reality!

"Ask and you shall receive; seek and you shall find; knock and the door will be opened to you. For everyone who asks will receive, and anyone who seeks will find and the door will be opened to those who knock." (Matthew 7:7-8)

Do not say to the universe, "*Please, universe, send me more money!"* Why not? Because what you are sending out into the universe is that at this point in time, you do not have enough money!

Instead say, "*Thank you universe for the money you are sending me! I am open to receive!"*

What is the difference?

The universe mirrors your thoughts, and reflects them back to you, manifested. Fact!

So the difference is, that while the universe replies to the first request with "*Yes that's right, you do not have enough money*", the second request on the other hand, illicits the reply from the universe, "*Yes, that's right I am sending you more money!*" And immediately a set of synchronised circumstances is being put in place to get that money to you!

There is no time in the universe outside of this physical earth plane. The universe does not recognise the future, as we see it. Everything is in the present, happening right here and now!

And, as we have seen, you cannot access this state of abundance if you see yourself as separate from God! You cannot access this state of abundance if you are still in the material earth consciousness. Your consciousness needs to be raised above the mortal, material dense consciousness in order to access the state of abundance.

So, if we create our own reality and if we live in an abundant universe, then why is there so much suffering, poverty and misery in this world?

The ultimate question!

And the ultimate untruth, the ultimate lie, is the belief that God has done all this!

The limiting conditions presently found and prevailing on this planet have not been created by God.

But if God creates everything, then surely God must have created all this too?

Well, actually, the answer is no! And a very profound no!

God creates, yes! And we humans are part of that creation. We humans are co-creators with the God Energy. But we have been endowed with free will! And it is our rampant misuse of that free will that has brought about the current conditions on planet earth. Every right, every privilege carries with it a responsibility. In this case, our gift of free will carries with it the responsibility to use the God Energy allotted to us wisely. But we have failed to do so. God cannot interfere in our free will. Neither can Jesus. Nor can any being from the higher vibrational energy frequency networks.

The ultimate truth is that the limiting conditions found on this planet are completely and entirely the creation of the humans inhabiting this planet. So it follows logically that if we desire to reverse these conditions then the only way in which this can possibly happen is by the human race taking responsibility for our own actions and deciding that we will create abundance and plenty instead of deprivation and scarcity. And this will only happen when a critical mass of people on this planet ascend to a higher level of consciousness, a higher level of consciousness than the present mortal, limited state of consciousness, and accept the perfection of God's creation rather than the imperfections created by man's free will.

And the reason why Jesus came to earth 2,000 years ago, the reason for Jesus reincarnating yet again on the earth plane was to call us up higher, to call us up into a higher state of consciousness than the mortal, limited, material consciousness into which so many people had allowed themselves to fall.

"Come, follow me!"

Follow Jesus to where?

To a higher state of consciousness! To the place he was already at! To the energy level of the Christ Consciousness! The same Christ Consciousness which is within each and every one of us! To the place we too can reach, just like him!

How different all this is from the teachings of orthodox religions! Orthodox religions that have deified and made Jesus into an idol! Orthodox religions that have taught that we will never get to where Jesus is! Orthodox religions that have denied us our rightful, natural birth right as sparks of the God Energy. Orthodox religions that have taught that Jesus is so far above and beyond us mere mortal beings that none of us could ever possibly follow in his footsteps! But that is exactly what Jesus invited us to do! And orthodox religions that have taught only the Divinity of Jesus, and have failed to teach the Divinity of man.

But! "Are ye not Gods?"

Jesus' own words!

But words which the early church fathers and those who edited the gospels overlooked, and in their sloppy editing, neglected to take out!

In just the same way as they neglected to remove Jesus' words about teaching to two different levels:

"Jesus preached his messages to the people, using many other parables like these; he told them as much as they could understand. He would not speak to them without using parables, but when he was alone with his disciples, he would explain everything to them." (Mark 4:33-34)

"Then the disciples came to Jesus and asked him, 'Why do you use parables when you talk to the people?'

Jesus answered. 'The knowledge about the secrets of the Kingdom of heaven has been given to you, but not to them. For the person who has something will be given more, so that he will have more than enough; but the person who has nothing will have taken away from him even the little he has. The reason I use parables in talking to them is that they look, but do not see, and they listen, but do not hear.' " (Matthew 13:10-13)

Obviously, Jesus had teachings, inner teachings, designed for the consciousness level of those further along their spiritual path and therefore open to more profound in-depth meanings, and also outer teachings, teachings designed for the majority of the population, those on a lower level of consciousness, and therefore not yet ready to hear those more profound, inner teachings.

And what a difference time makes! Today, 2,000 years later, the situation has changed dramatically! It is completely different! There are millions of people today ready and willing to receive the inner teachings of Jesus.

We have been deprived of those inner teachings of Jesus for all this time by orthodox religions who set themselves up as intermediaries between us and God!

But Jesus sowed the seeds that have germinated, the seeds that are now sprouting, the seeds that are now bursting.

Where?

In our higher state of consciousness, of course! That's where the fertile ground is! And that is the only place where we can hear Jesus' inner teachings! No place else!

The Law of Forgiveness and Non-Judgement

We must forgive. We are duty bound to forgive. We need to forgive.

And why do we need to forgive?

We need to forgive not only because of the universal law that specifies that what we send out we get back; we need to forgive not only because of the universal law of karma and we need to forgive not only because according to how we forgive others, we too will equally be forgiven. Or not!

We need to forgive too, for another reason, probably the most important reason.

We need to forgive, because in forgiving, we release ourselves from the weight of anger we are carrying around with us, like a heavy sack around our neck, pulling us down, down, down. When we forgive, we can feel that weight taking flight. The anger leaves. We are freeing ourselves from all that pain and misery!

And we must not judge. When we judge others, we are judging appearances. But appearances are just that, - appearances. Appearances mask the reality underneath. Appearances are just the physical, the material, masking the underlying spiritual.

Jesus tells us:

"Stop judging by external standards, and judge by true standards." (John 7:24)

When you judge others, you inevitably condemn yourself to living a life based on superficial knowledge and incomplete assumptions. If you see the appearances in others as the reality, then you are basing your life on the mere visible, rather than the hidden, underlying spiritual. We do not know what any one else's life plan is, so we cannot judge! When you forgive, you rid yourself of the crushing burden of hate that is hanging around your neck!

The key is to see yourself and everyone else as divine light, then you will not judge, you will not condemn, you will send them only love and light!

*"But now I tell you: love your enemies and pray for those who persecute you, so that you may become the children of your Father in heaven. For he makes his sun to shine on bad and good people alike, and gives rain to those who do good and to those who do evil ." (*Matthew 5: 46-47)

We are all one. I am you and you are me! How can I condemn you if I am condemning myself in the process?

"*Do not judge others, so that God will not judge you, for God will judge you in the same way as you judge others, and he will apply to you the same rules you apply to others. Why, then, do you look at the speck in your brother's eye, and pay no attention to the log in your own eye? How dare you say to your brother, ' Please, let me take that speck out of our eye,' when you have a log in your own eye? You hypocrites! First take the log out of your own eye, and then you will be able to see clearly to take the speck out of your brother's eye.*" (Matthew 7:1-5)

When someone hurts us, reacting with vengeance and more of the same is not the answer. It is **AN** answer, but it is not **THE** answer.

Jesus' contemporaries were obsessed with the law and adherence to the law. They were all into what they called justice, acting according to the precepts of the law. But justice does not do forgiveness. Justice does punishment through an eye for an eye and a tooth for a tooth. But Jesus had come to teach love, pity and forgiveness.

An eye for an eye and a tooth for a tooth! That only leaves us all blind and toothless! Charming! What good is that going to do anyone? We can only disarm anger and hatred with love and light, not with more of the same. Those who live by the sword die by the sword.

Look at it like this.

The icy north wind and the sun are having an argument about

which of them is the stronger. They decide to have a competition to test their various strengths. They spy a man walking along the road. The icy, bitter north wind claims that he can get the man's coat off him where the sun cannot. So he blows and blows. The man wraps his coat closer around him, buffeted by the wind. The icy north wind blows harder, to his maximum strength, angrily tearing at the man's coat in a desperate attempt to be the victor. But the harder and the more fierce he blows, the more tightly the man pulls his coat around him. Eventually the icy, bitter north wind is forced to admit defeat.

Now it is the sun's turn. The sun starts to shine, and shine and shine, increasing the brightness and the heat. Lovingly, he beams down. The man starts to release his tight hold on his coat. The sun shines stronger. The man opens his coat buttons. The sun increases the heat and the light. The man, sweat pouring down his forehead, finally takes off his coat with a gasp of relief.

Get the message?

Love and light and warmth will always succeed where anger, bitterness and coldness will always fail.

And yes, we must "*turn the other cheek*"*!* As we shall see in the final chapter, this does not mean turning our face to get another blow. This means turning our other identity, our other side, while at the same time staying in our higher consciousness level and not allowing ourselves to descend to the lower consciousness level where that person who had offended us must be.

That higher consciousness level where Jesus was, when he could say, even as he was dying:

"Father forgive them, for they know not what they do."

Jesus was the master of psychology and he knew the formula, he knew the secret. In order to forgive, we must be in a higher vibrational consciousness than the person who has offended us or wronged us. Someone who is spiritually bankrupt, spiritually closed or spiritually impoverished is incapable of forgiveness. What they want is revenge and retribution. And the fact that this is what they want signifies that they are in the lower state of consciousness. So they need our pity, our compassion, simply because, compared to the joyous splendour of our life in the higher consciousness, their life seems so squalid and dark. Stay in your higher consciousness, in your higher vantage point, and do not give into the temptation to retaliate with like, because you will only be pulled down to their level, which is exactly what they want!

The Laws of Karma and Reincarnation

After all this talk about forgiveness, we now need to consider the following.

God does not forgive. Fact!

What? After all we have just read about forgiveness? God does not forgive?

Let me explain!

Why does God not forgive?

God does not forgive simply because God does not need to forgive! Fact!

And why does God not need to forgive?

God does not need to forgive because there is nothing for God to forgive! Fact!

And why is there nothing for God to forgive?

There is nothing for God to forgive simply because the Law of Karma takes care of all that! Fact!

Karma is not a punishment. It is a balancing of the less-than-good deeds we do with the good deeds we do. For each and every one of us, with no exception, our good deeds gather good karma, while our less-than good deeds incur bad karma. Bad karma is simply misused energy. And our good karma balances out our bad karma.

As we have already seen, everything that exists in the entire world of form is created from the God energy. Everything that we do is done with God's energy. Every deed, every word, every thought goes out from us in the form of energy, which is then mirrored by the universe and returned to us magnified.

Once we send out energy in the form of our thoughts, words or deeds, then we ourselves cannot recall that energy. We cannot press the delete button and wipe it out. We have begun a process which will unfold in time. A process which is designed to inevitably return to us.

That's the bad news!

And the good news is?

The good news is that, even though we ourselves cannot recall, delete or destroy that energy once we have sent it out, we can still change it. Energy cannot be killed or destroyed. But it can be changed, it can be transmuted.

So how, if we cannot delete or destroy energy, are we going to be able to change it?

Look at it this way. Let's say, for example, you hate someone and you are angry with them. You are now sending out energy in your feelings of anger and hatred for that person. That energy you are sending out is negative, heavy low vibrational energy. That energy, being a negative, heavy, low vibrational energy, travels at a slower speed than high frequency energy sent out by good thoughts. Travelling at a slower rate, that energy might return to you in a number of years, or it might trundle on in to another life-time. But one thing for sure! It is definitely on its way back to you! You might think you have got away with what you have done, but you are only deluding yourself. Karma is a universal law! What you send out, you get back! You must balance your not-so-good deeds with your good deeds. You must balance your misuse of energy! No one escapes! There is no way out! We are all locked into the grinding, inexorable wheel of karma!

Now, in the meantime, whilst your bad karma is working its way back to you, you realise what you have done is wrong. You have hurt or maligned another person. You admit your wrong-doing and you deeply regret it. So you now send out feelings of love towards that same person.

Now what have you just done? You have now sent out energy in the form of love and acknowledgment of your wrong-doing. That energy you are now sending out is a positive, light, high vibrational frequency energy. That energy, being a positive, light, high frequency energy, travels at a much faster speed than the negative, heavy, low vibrational frequency energy you sent out previously, and which is still in the process of working its way back to you.

See what is happening? The lighter higher frequency energy you have just sent out is catching up with the previous heavy, low frequency energy you sent out simply because it is travelling at a much faster speed. At the point of catch-up, that higher, lighter energy superimposes itself on the heavier low frequency energy, changing it so it can no longer return to you as bad karma! You have managed to get it absorbed into the lighter, higher energy you sent out after it! It no longer exists as bad karma! You have paid off that particular debt of karma!

Now you are probably thinking, how come the heavier energy does not absorb the lighter energy? Surely, as it is the heavier, it should be doing the absorbing instead of being absorbed?

Well, think of a dark room. When you go into a dark room, how do you get rid of the dark? By gathering it all up and shoving it into a bag? Which you then dispose of?

Hardly!

You turn on the light! And hey presto! The darkness disappears! It becomes absorbed in the light!

Get the picture?

It's exactly the same with good and bad karma! The good karma, travelling faster, can catch up with the bad karma and change its form from bad to good. The bad energy Is transmuted, changed. The energy still exists, because remember, energy never dies! But it no longer exists as bad energy. That's gone, gone for good! Literally, gone for good! It is now good energy! And why? Simply because you changed your thoughts! That's how powerful your thoughts really are!

But wait! This does not mean that you can send out as much dark energy as you like and get rid of all your pent-up feelings of anger, spite, jealousy, whatever, in one go, and then immediately say you are sorry and send out light energy in order to catch up with and absorb that dark energy! Not at all!

It's what is in your heart that counts! And what is in your heart, you might well be able to keep concealed from other people, but you cannot conceal that which is in your heart from yourself or from the spirit world. So in actual fact, because of your ulterior motives, you have now incurred more bad karma! A hurricane is heading for you, a cyclone, a tsunami even! When it will hit land is anyone's guess, but it will hit! And you know what? You sure will feel it!

And it's because of the law of karma that God does not need to forgive. Karma is actually the safety mechanism built inherently into man's free will. Without this in-built safety mechanism, man's abuse of free will would run rampant! Man would destroy himself, destroy the earth and destroy the rest of the entire cosmos.

So thank God for karma! It is karma that keeps us all in control!

Karma trundles down through history, lifetime after lifetime, like a World War One tank, like a steamroller, like a juggernaut without a braking mechanism, affecting each and every one of us! Karma has no favorites. There is no favouritism or discrimination with karma! There are no exceptions to the rule or the Law of Karma!

And karma is intrinsically bound up with reincarnation.

Death, reincarnation and karma are all inter-connected, all inter-twined, all inter-related, and all designed to teach us to move away from materiality and toward our true nature. What we do not balance in this lifetime, we will balance in the next lifetime or in some other future lifetime. We will return to earth in an endless cycle of birth, death and re-birth until we have learned to control our use of energy! Because it is our misuse of energy that has brought bad karma on us in the first place!

We are all destined for perfection, for sainthood, whether we like it or not! Life is all about the process of evolution. And evolution is just that, - a process. Evolution just does not happen in one short life-time! Even if we manage to live to be well over one hundred!

We have seen that bad karma is misused energy, and we have seen too that all your bad karma must be balanced with your good karma. Because you have misused this energy in this material world, you are therefore tied to this material world until you balance it out, as you cannot access the spiritual energy vibrational levels carrying your bad karma with you. So your soul must continue to reincarnate time and time again in this material world in order to get a chance to balance your karma.

All wrong or hurtful acts, thoughts or words are coming from a certain state of consciousness. So, obviously, you need to raise your state of consciousness in order to end the cycle you have established for yourself of life after life on the karmic wheel. And when you end that cycle, when you finally balance your karma, you then have access to the spiritual energy vibrational levels. At last! At last you are on your way up the cosmic spiritual elevator! You are on your way to sainthood!

So what did Jesus teach about reincarnation?

Jesus himself obviously believed in reincarnation because he was affiliated with the Essene community at Qumran, and according to Josephus, the first-century Jewish historian, the Essenes believed in reincarnation. Jesus, in the gospels, does not actually mention the word reincarnation at all. But the idea, the concept, the belief in reincarnation is there, when we look for it.

In actual fact, there are several passages in the gospels that can only be understood if they are considered against the background of the belief in reincarnation.

Jesus himself said:

"Before Abraham was born, I am". (John 8:58)

But those listening did not understand what Jesus meant and took up stones to throw at him.

We have earlier heard what Jesus said to Nicodemus:

"I am telling you the truth: no one can see the Kingdom of God without being born again.'

'How can a grown man be born again?' Nicodemus asked. 'He certainly cannot enter his mother's womb and be born a second time!'

'I am telling you the truth', replied Jesus. 'No one can enter the Kingdom of God without being born of water and the Spirit. A Person is born physically of human parents but is born spiritually of the Spirit. Do not be surprised because I tell you that you must all be born again. The wind blows wherever it wishes; you hear the sound it makes, but you do not know where it comes from or where it is going. It is like that with everyone who is born of the Spirit.'

'How can this be?' answered Nicodemus.

Jesus answered, 'You are a great teacher in Israel, and you don't know this? I am telling you the truth: we speak of what we know and report what we have seen, yet none of you is willing to accept our message. You do not believe me when I tell you about the things of this world; how will you ever believe me then, when I tell you about the things of heaven?' " (John 3:1-13)

According to Josephus, and as we have already seen, the Pharisees, the founders of rabbinic Judaism believed in reincarnation. Josephus wrote that the Pharisees believed that the souls of good men are '*removed into other bodies'* and will '*have power to revive and live again'*. On the other hand, the Sadducees, the other prominent sect in Jewish Palestine, as we have also seen earlier, did not emphasise life after death and maintained '*there is no resurrection*', (Matthew 22-23). So we can deduce from this that the Sadducees did not believe in reincarnation.

Jesus himself asked his disciples:

"Who do people say I am?"

And the answer they gave him?

"Some say that you are John the Baptist, but others Elijah, and still others say that you are Jeremiah or one of the prophets." (Mark

8:27-28)

Surely this answer Jesus' disciples gave him confirms their belief in reincarnation! How could they otherwise have said he was someone who was long dead?

Then there is the account of Jesus healing the blind man:

"As Jesus was walking along, he saw a man who had been born blind. His disciples asked him, 'Teacher, whose sin caused him to be born blind? Was it his own or his parents' sin?' (John 9:1)

How could this man possibly have sinned in his mother's womb before he was born? Impossible! Except of course, unless you believe that the man had a previous life.

After the Transfiguration, the disciples asked Jesus:

"Why do the teachers of the Law say that Elijah has to come first?'

'Elijah is indeed coming first', answered Jesus, 'and he will get everything ready. But I tell you that Elijah has already come and the people did not recognise him, but treated him just as they pleased. In the same way they will also ill-treat the Son of Man.'

Then the disciples understood that he was talking to them about John the Baptist." (Matthew 17:10-11)

How could John the Baptist suddenly have come again? John the Baptist was born in the same way any other child coming into this earth plane was born. Therefore, he must have reincarnated as John the Baptist, having previously been Elijah. The prophet who was Elijah chose to reincarnate as John the Baptist at the same time as Jesus, in order to support Jesus in his mission.

At the beginning of Christianity, reincarnation was one of the main pillars of church teaching and was an uncontested fact until the fourth century. Actually, the idea is found in the oldest traditions of Western civilization, as well as being taught throughout the ancient Near East and Orient.

Josephus records in his *Jewish War* (3, 8, 5) and in his *Antiquities of the Jews* (18, 1, 3) that reincarnation was taught widely in his day, while his contemporary in Alexandria, Philo Judaeus, in various parts of his writings, also refers to the same soul being re-embodied in one form or another.

So too, the second and third generations of Christian Church Fathers taught about reincarnation. Justin Martyr (100-I65 C.E), St. Clement of Alexandria (150-220 C.E.) and Origen (185-254 C.E.) all taught the pre-existence of souls, taking up reincarnation or one or another aspect of re-embodiment. Origin, in his '*Contra Celsum*' asks: "*Is it not rational that souls should be introduced into bodies, in accordance with their merits and previous deeds?*" (Contra Celsum 1, xxxii) Saint Jerome (340-420 C.E.), translator of the Latin version of the Bible known as the '*Vulgate*', in his Letter to Demetrias (a Roman matron), states that some Christian sects in his day taught a form of reincarnation as an esoteric doctrine, imparting it to a few *"as a traditional truth which was not to be divulged."* Synesis, Bishop of Ptolemais (370-480 C.E.) also taught about reincarnation and in one of his prayers wrote: "*Father, grant that my soul may merge into the light, and be no more thrust back into the illusion of earth."*

The concept of reincarnation seeped down through history to the medieval ages. Saint Francis of Assisi (1182-1226), founder of the Franciscans, taught about it. Henry More, (1614-1687), the noted clergyman of the Church of England wrote a long essay titled '*The Immortality of the Soul*' in which he wrote: "*There was never any philosopher that held the soul spiritual and immortal but he held also that it did pre-exist."* And in his poem '*A Platonick Song of the Soul*' he wrote: "*I would sing the Prae-existency / Of humane souls, and live once o'er again / By recollection and quick memory / All that is past since first we all began."*

Reincarnation was condemned by Christian church fathers in 553 C.E. during the reign of Justinius, the emperor of Byzantine, the

Eastern Roman Empire.

In 451, the Council of Chalcedon (the Fourth Ecumenical Council) had declared that Jesus was both human and divine and persecuted those who failed to acquiesce. Justinius was later one of the most zealous persecutors.

It was actually Justinius' wife, Theodora, who was the real instigator of the condemnation of reincarnation. Theodora had risen rapidly through the social ranks from prostitute to concubine to emperor's wife through a combination of cunning wiles and schemes. The supreme opportunist, and not content with worldly gains, Theodora planned her own deification. And reincarnation stood in her way of deification. Reincarnation meant that she would come back again and again to this earthly plane to balance her evil deeds. Being reborn simply negated the possibility of being deified. As long as people believed in reincarnation, they would never accept Theodoro as a goddess. And so the concept of reincarnation was banned when Theodora convened the Synod of the Eastern Church of Constantinople in 543 C.E.

Today, in this the twenty-first century, reincarnation is spoken of much more openly and widely than in more recent modern centuries. Many people are remembering past experiences which could only have happened in a previous life-time and recognising certain places when they visit them for the first time. Children in particular can vividly recall past life-times.

Reincarnation makes sense of what would otherwise be an extremely non-sensical situation. It is logical and sensible to believe that each and every one of us will reap the rewards of what we sow, and suffer the punishment for our misdeeds, our misuse of energy. If only this concept had been retained over the last centuries, then our present world would not be in its current mess. If only it had been brought home to us that we never get away with any misuse of energy, then history would have taken a very different route.

"People will reap exactly what they sow. If they sow in the field of their natural desires, from it they will gather the harvest of death; if they sow in the field of the Spirit, from the Spirit they will gather the harvest of eternal life." (Galatians 6:7)

So there you have it!

We all face our own karma, whether for good or for bad, according to our own freely chosen actions, our own freely chosen use or misuse of energy.

Jesus cannot save us from our own freely-chosen actions! God cannot save us from our own misuse of the energy allotted to us in each life-time! No more than can the church confessional!

Each of us, alone, is responsible for our own actions, and each of us, alone, must face the consequences of those freely-chosen actions. We are all subject to karma, no exceptions, what we put out is what we get back! We reap what we sow! No Jesus, no God, no church can save us or protect us from karma! It trundles down through history, catching each one of us! There is no escape! That is one of the greatest Spiritual laws!

No Jesus or God can forgive us our misdeeds and wipe the slate clean for us! We cannot buy our way into the higher vibrational energy frequencies of the spirit world. We must earn our own way, through living a life of unconditional love and compassion for our fellow travellers, at one with all of creation, at one in the Great Universal Consciousness. There is no judgment by God, Jesus or anyone else. We face our own life review each and every time we return to Spirit after our earthly sojourn and it is then we ourselves will feel the pain that we caused to any other form of life while on our journey here. No matter how many indulgences we gain here from the Church, no matter how many masses we pay to get said for us, no matter how much we donate to charity, we are still solely responsible for our own spirituality and the way in which we live our life. No last minute forgiveness or reprieve by the church will make any difference whatsoever when we face our own life review! No last minute forgiveness or reprieve by the church will get us any further up the cosmic elevator to a higher energy vibrational energy, beyond that level which we have earned for ourselves. No last minute reprieve or forgiveness by the church will save us from facing our own karma!

The BEATITUDES

The Beatitudes or **BE ATTITUDES** are eight blessings recounted fully in the Sermon on the Mount in the Gospel of Matthew (5:3-10) and in a shorter version in the gospel of Luke (6:17-49) Each of the Beatitudes is a proverb-like proclamation.

The Beatitudes are in sharp contrast to the Ten Commandments given to Moses on Mount Sinai and recounted in the Old Testament Book of Exodus. These Ten Commandments are ten strong, no-arguing imperatives "*Thou shalt not!*", listing the evils one must avoid in daily life if one wants to enter the Kingdom of Heaven.

The message of Jesus in the Beatitudes on the other hand, is one of humility, charity and brotherly love.

And, like all his other teachings and messages, there is an inner meaning to each of them. They reiterate the message that we must care for our immortal Spiritual body rather that our temporary physical body. Jesus was trying to get the message across to the first century Palestinian Jews who were expecting the imminent arrival in this world of a Messiah who would rescue them from Roman rule, that the Kingdom they awaited is not of this world, but of a higher energy vibrational frequency level altogether, that which we see as Heaven.

First, we must consider what the word "*blessed*" means. The Greek word translated "*blessed*" can also be translated "*happy*". The idea is that a person will have joy. The blessedness is from God's perspective, not from our human perspective. It connotates a spiritual prosperity, a spiritual happiness, a spiritual joy and not necessarily a human or an earthly joy or happiness.

So in this light, many of the Beatitudes appear contradictory and paradoxical.

The first Beatitude, "*Blessed are the poor in spirit, for theirs is the kingdom of heaven*" is certainly one such. How, we ask, can one be poor in spirit and attain the kingdom of Heaven? Is this not contradicting all we have learned about the inner teachings of Jesus so far? Surely it would be those who are rich in spirit who will inherit the kingdom of Heaven?

Again, we need to go beneath the surface, we need to probe deeper, in order to get the real, the inner meaning.

Orthodox religion has always advocated poverty as a virtue. But we have just seen in the section on abundance that it is not a sin to be rich and that richness and abundance is our natural right. So how do we reconcile this with the first Beatitude?

"*Poor in spirit"* actually means to be humble. Humble in the sense that we take no credit for anything, acknowledging that all comes from the God Source. No ego! No pride! No puffed-up importance! No looking for elevation, reward or fame! Pride interferes with the God energy getting through to us, because we are blocked. Blocked by the negative desires of anger and seeking revenge if we are offended. Blocked by the negative dictates of our own ego.

It means becoming like a child again, emptying yourself of the desire to exercise your own personal will and becoming devoid of pre-conceived ideas, pre-conceived concepts, pre-conceived notions. It means being willing to be open-minded to the truth and being willing to accept that truth. It means stripping away all the baggage that we carry with us in the form of our strongly held beliefs, and being able to fill that vacuum with truthful spiritual teachings.

If we could all just be humble, rid ourselves of the ego, and therefore become poor in spirit, there would be no such thing as war.

The second Beatitude is, "*Blessed are they who mourn, for they shall be comforted".* Again, orthodox religion has advocated suffering as a virtue. But again, there is an inner meaning!

Mourning in this context is a blessing, because as we progress up the Spiritual ladder, the more we ascend in truth, the more we realise our Christ-Self, our likeness to God, our divine origins, then we mourn because of how we used to be and the time we wasted, and we mourn for those who have not yet caught on to the reality of their divine nature. So, the fact that we mourn is actually a good sign that we have progressed spiritually to a higher level of realisation.

Furthermore, it is through challenges that we reach our destination of a higher state of consciousness. Challenges present us with lessons to learn. They may be difficult lessons, but they are all the better for that. So every great challenge or problem that we face is a blessing in disguise.

The third Beatitude is "*Blessed are the meek, for they shall inherit the earth*". This too, seems contradictory. How can those who are meek and mild take over the earth? Surely it is the bullies and the aggressive, volatile, mercurial, belligerent people who take over the earth?

So what does "*Blessed are the meek*" mean? What does it mean that the meek are blessed? The word "*meek*" is translated from the Greek word '*praeis*', and means mildness, humility, or gentleness of spirit. Meekness is humility towards God and towards all others. It means having the right to do something, but refraining from exercising that right for the benefit of someone else. It means exercising patience and restraint.

Meekness is a state of consciousness. A state of consciousness which enables us to realise our limitations as physical beings, and our strength in our divine resources. Our real strength lies in our divine intuition, our God ideas, rather than our human ideas. Meekness models the humility of Jesus. Much like saying we remain calm when provoked, and think first before we react.

The fourth Beatitude is, "*Blessed are they who hunger and thirst for righteousness, for they shall be satisfied*". The key to this Beatitude lies in our understanding of the word *"righteousness"*. We, in our limited human thinking and understanding take righteousness to mean being seen to be doing the right thing. Obeying the laws, standing up for our rights, being seen praying, all constitute support for what we consider to be righteous.

But that's not what Jesus meant! Jesus was talking about our inner attitudes. Justice and righteousness can only come about as a result of knowing the truth. This brings us back to an earlier chapter, and the meaning of "*The truth shall set you free".* The truth does not entail mere observance of the law, but the understanding of our divine nature and the continuous desire for justice and moral perfection, which will in turn lead us to a raising of our vibrational energy, a raising of our spiritual consciousness, our spiritual awareness. If you hunger and thirst for anything, you will head towards the goal you have in mind. But you must first desire it greatly. To "*hunger and thirst for righteousness"* means to be greatly and fervently desirous of attaining spiritual truths. If we seek these spiritual truths and teachings with all our mind and heart, then we will be given them, they will be revealed to us. But we have first got to desire them as they cannot be forced upon us. We must ask.

The fifth Beatitude is, "*Blessed are the merciful, for they shall obtain mercy".* This Beatitude is reminiscent of the teaching about what you give out you get back. This is known as the law of consciousness. And the law of consciousness dictates that life is lived from the inside outwards. The only way you have any control over changing the world around you is to change yourself by changing your inner thoughts, because the universe mirrors your thoughts.

Jesus is teaching us here that it is our own state of consciousness that attracts things to us. If we do not like what we are getting, then we need to change our consciousness in order to change what is coming to us. In other words, we create our own reality, we create our own world. What we do to others, we attract back to ourselves.

There are corporal works of mercy, and there are spiritual works of mercy. Corporal works of mercy include feeding the hungry; providing drink to the thirsty; clothing the naked; sheltering the homeless; comforting those in prison; visiting the sick and burying the dead. Spiritual works of mercy include advising sinners;

teaching the uninformed; counselling the doubtful; comforting those who are sorrowful; being patient with those who error; forgiving offenses and praying for the living and for the dead.

Mercy is love, compassion and forgiveness in action. And just as we send those out, so we will get back in return.

Jesus told us:

"*Whatsoever you do to one of these, the least of my brethren you do it to me.*" (Matthew 25:31-46)

There is that constant message, in front of us time and time again! What message? The message that we are all one! I am you and you are me! We are all united in the Oneness of the great God Energy. United with Jesus!

The sixth Beatitude is *"Blessed are the pure of heart, for they shall see God".* So who are these "*pure of heart*"?

These pure of heart are those who perform kind acts purely out of unconditional love, seeking no personal or monetary gain, no acclaim or even any sort of acknowledgment. To be pure of heart means to be free of all self-seeking desires and selfish intentions. To be pure of heart means to view all things from the God perspective, and not from our limited human perspective. To perform any act completely and perfectly free of any intention of personal gain or personal advantage is an act of pure, unconditional love. And pure and selfless giving guarantees happiness! To all concerned! Everyone's a winner!

And being pure in heart was what Jesus meant when he said '*Unless you become as little children, you cannot enter the kingdom of heaven.*"

Children are pure light and love, uncontaminated as yet by the ways of this dense earth energy. They have a foot in both worlds for the first seven or so years of their earthly life. They live totally in the present, taking joy in all around them. They do not discriminate between playmates, but gravitate towards all colours and creeds. They are the epitome of purity in heart.

The seventh Beatitude is "*Blessed are the peacemakers, for they shall be called the children of God"*. But are we not all *"children of God"?* Jesus told us: *"Peace I leave with you: My peace I give unto you". (*John 14:27) But you cannot give that which you yourself do not have!

To be a peacemaker, or to bring peace to other people, you must first dwell in peace yourself.

And how does one dwell in peace?

One dwells in peace by acknowledging the God in oneself and in all other forms of life. Such an acknowledgement precludes judgement or criticism of any kind whatsoever towards any other person. Such an acknowledgement guarantees a sending out and forth of unconditional love, and unconditional love only. You are free from spite, envy, anger, jealousy, hatred or desire for revenge.

And there is only one state of being as a result!

The state of dwelling in peace!

If only we could all just see this, if only we could all just visualise this, then there would be no such thing as war!

The process begins with each and every one of us, individually. Remember, you cannot pass on to anyone else what you yourself do not have! First you must establish the state of peace within yourself and then, and only then can you start to be a peacemaker. Remember! Life is lived from the inside outwards!

The eighth Beatitude is "*Blessed are they who are persecuted for the sake of righteousness, for theirs is the kingdom of heaven"*.

This is elaborated on further:

"Blessed are you when men revile you and persecute you and utter all kinds of evil against you falsely on my account. rejoice and be

glad, for your reward is great in heaven, for so men persecuted the prophets who were before you." (Matthew 5:11-12)

This Beatitude has been greatly misunderstood for the last 2,000 years. It is not advocating martyrdom as a way into heaven. As with everything, there is an outer meaning and an inner meaning.

Jesus spelt the outer meaning out clearly to his followers:

"If they persecute me, they will persecute you." (John 15:20-21)

Nearly all of Jesus' disciples suffered persecution. The rest, including Mary Magdalene and Joseph of Arimathea were forced to flee for their lives.

But the inner meaning is referring to the persecution of the mind through temptation. Again Jesus was referring to attitude here, and our process of thinking. He is talking about temptation which comes to the minds of all of us. There is nothing wrong with being tempted! We all in fact need temptation, because it is through being tempted that we overcome temptation and evolve spiritually. It is through being tempted that we awaken to our spiritual being. If we were not being tempted then that would be a bad sign! That would mean that we are living in such a negative state that we do not need temptation!

Even Jesus himself was tempted. So temptation is good for us. It strengthens us and gives us a deeper awareness.

So we can see that the Beatitudes, as taught by Jesus were based on humility, charity and brotherly love.

Pope Francis, during his visit to Sweden in November 2016, proposed a modern set of 6 new Beatitudes based on these same Beatitudes of Jesus:

"Blessed are those who remain faithful while enduring evils inflicted on them by others and forgive them from their heart."

"Blesses are those who look into the eyes of the abandoned and

marginalised and show them their closeness."

"Blessed are those who see God in every person and strive to make others also discover him."

"Blessed are those who protect and care for our common home."

"Blessed are those who renounce their own comfort in order to help others."

"Blessed are those who pray and work for full communion between Christians."

These may have been written for a very different world than the world Jesus knew 2,000 years ago, but as we can see, they are still based on the teachings of Jesus, the teachings of humility, charity and brotherly love.

The Lord's Prayer

What you are about to read now may well shock some of you. And I understand that. I really do! We have been programmed for so long now and our long-held beliefs are hard to shift. Many of us feel we should not even be questioning what we have been taught! If I had written a few centuries ago what I am now writing, my guts would have been had for garters! And by none other than you-know-who! But this is 2017 and we are rapidly moving from a fear based approach to life, with all its incumbent violence, hatred and guilt, to a heart centered approach to life, where we spread unconditional love and compassion, knowing that we are all one and that there is no separation from us and the divine energy that is God.

Jesus told us to pray. And he taught us the Lord's Prayer. But we seem to have got his message all wrong! Yet again!

When we pray, we are usually reciting glibly repeated learned words and phrases which we have been taught from our early years. But that is not what Jesus meant by prayer! Not at all!

Now I am not for one minute saying that a large group of people praying together is not effective. It is extremely effective! But not in the way we seem to think!

Remember what we read about energy and how our words and thoughts go out as forms of energy and attract the same back to us?

Well, the energy generated by people praying in large numbers is magnified many times greater than one person praying alone, and attracts back a much greater energy in return.

But it is ***how*** we pray that we must now consider.

Prayer is an inner conversation with God, with our own Higher Self, and our own Higher Self has the answers to all the questions we could ever ask. Remember! God is within each and every one of us! God is not an external figure to whom we make our requests hoping they will somehow be granted.

So with all this in mind, let us now look at The Lord's Prayer:

"Our Father who art in heaven / Hallowed be thy name / Thy kingdom come , thy will be done on earth as it is in heaven / Give us this day our daily bread / And forgive us our trespasses as we forgive those who trespass against us / and lead us not into temptation / But deliver us from evil / Amen"

We are all spiritual travellers, all on different stages of our journey, all at different points on the road. So I ask you to bear with me as we now look at the inner meanings behind the Lord's Prayer.

We have always seen this prayer as a set of supplications, asking God to bestow certain blessings on us.

But God does not have what we want or need! And why not? Simply because God is actually the substance of that want or need! Get the message?

The key to getting what we need or desire, as we have seen throughout this entire book, is to raise your consciousness to the level where we see the wholeness of life within ourselves, where we see ourselves as God made manifest. God is everything. God is everything we could ever ask for.

Jesus, throughout the gospels, gives us affirmations, not supplications. In fact, his prayers were mostly affirmations:

"I AM the light of the world......... I AM the truth....... I AM the good shepherd........ I AM the way.......I Am the bread of life..... I AM the resurrection and the life.......I and the Father ARE one...... I AM come that they may have life and that they might have it more abundantly.........."

So what is the difference between affirmations and supplications?

A supplication is a request, an asking, a beseeching for something to be granted to us. A supplication immediately and automatically has connotations that the person whom we are addressing is an external force, a force outside of ourselves.

An affirmation, on the other hand, connotates that whatever it is about which we are speaking already is in existence and already is within us.

So let us now look at the words of the Lord's Prayer in a different light. Let us now look at them as if they are a set of affirmations rather than supplications as we have always been taught:

*"Our Father, you **ARE** in heaven. Your name **IS** hallowed. Thy*

kingdom ***IS*** *come. Thy will* ***IS*** *done on earth as it is in heaven. You* ***DO*** *give us our daily bread today and every day. You* ***DO*** *forgive us our trespasses, even as we forgive. You* ***DO NOT*** *lead us into temptation. You* ***DO*** *deliver us from evil."*

See the difference?

See the difference in the Lord's Prayer as a set of supplications and the Lord's Prayer as a powerful affirmation? A powerful acknowledgement prayer of thanks for what already is! A powerful prayer of gratitude!

And remember! The universe mirrors our words and thoughts!

Let us delve deeper!

"Your name **IS** *hallowed."* The word *hallowed* means *whole* and *perfect,* and the word *name* means *nature.* So this affirmation is an acknowledgement of the wholeness and perfection of God, and because God is in us, then we too are whole and perfect in our spiritual dimension, in our spiritual identity.

"Thy kingdom **IS** *come. Thy will* **IS** *done on earth as it is in heaven."* And what exactly is God's will? God's will is to create, and to create perfection through us. We are all going towards perfection, and when we say these words, we are simply confirming that this is already happening. We are acknowledging that we are God in manifestation, we are God in form, and we are an individualised expression of God. We must each use our individual, unique talents to bring about a better world, to propel earth forwards on its evolutionary path, to propel earth forwards towards perfection.

"You **DO** *give us our daily bread today and every day."* Bread is the food of life. And when we make this affirmation, we are acknowledging the fact that God is our constant supply of everything we need and desire. The universe is constantly giving us abundance and riches. Everything comes to us in a natural flow of universal energy. And because we are of the God essence, we only need to call everything to us from the over-flowing universe. We

must trust that we are always being looked after, no matter what, by a loving universe that knows our every need and desire.

"*You* **DO** *forgive us our trespasses, even as we forgive.*" Here is a direct reference to the concept that what we give out, we get back. This is one of the greatest universal and cosmic laws. As you sow, so shall you reap. This is very different from asking God's forgiveness in a supplication. Because, remember! God does not forgive! God does not need to forgive! Simply because karma, as we saw earlier, takes care of all that! Karma! The safety mechanism built into man's free will for everyone's protection!

"You **DO NOT** *lead us into temptation. You* **DO** *deliver us from evil."* We have always been led to believe that God does indeed lead us into temptation and difficulties. Temptation comes to us, not from an external source, but from within ourselves, from our own human ego. But we are of divine nature, we are of divine origin, we are of divine essence and when we are operating from this acknowledgement, then we are aware of the God presence within us, and that is our shield against evil.

So you see, the Lord's Prayer makes much more sense when we see it as a set of positive affirmations, rather than a set of supplications to an external source.

When we see it as a set of positive affirmations, what exactly are we doing?

We are acknowledging the God essence within ourselves. We are acknowledging that God is the source of all our provisions, through an over-abundant and giving universe. We are acknowledging the law of karma, and hence we are more aware of what we send out there in the form of our every word, thought and action.

What a wonderful prayer of gratitude and thanksgiving! And Jesus himself taught us that!

The Greatest Commandment is Love

"And now I give you a new commandment: love one another. As I have loved you, so you must love one another." (John 13:34)

" 'Teacher', he said, 'which is the greatest commandment in the Law?' Jesus answered: 'Love the Lord your God with all your heart, with all your soul, and with all your mind. This is the greatest and the most important commandment. The second most important commandment is like it: 'Love your neighbour as you love yourself'. The whole Law of Moses and the teachings of the prophets depend on these two commandments." (Matthew 22:36-40)

Love transcends all. Love conquers all. Love over-rides all.

Jesus constantly spoke about the importance of love.

But what did he mean? What is love? How do we show love?

We usually see love as having strings attached. We will love on condition of this or that. But when we attach conditions to love, then it is not love. That is manipulation. Manipulation masquerading as love for personal ends.

The one and only kind of love is unconditional love, and it is this unconditional love which Jesus constantly emphasised.

Unconditional love has no strings attached. We accept that person exactly as he is, because we see beneath the surface to the bright Spiritual light that is really there.

"Namaste!"

"The God in me acknowledges the God in you!"

If only we could put this into practice! If only we could see the beautiful Spiritual light under the appearance! If only we could accept each other and every other form of life as being of divine essence! Then we would not judge, we would not condemn, and we most certainly would not hurt, destroy or kill.

And we must see ourselves in the same beautiful Spiritual light. And because we see ourselves as the beautiful Spiritual light that each and every one of really is, then we accept ourselves as we really are, we do not carry guilt, we do not carry any sort of hatred towards ourselves, we treat ourselves with understanding, and we forgive ourselves for any wrong we have done to others.

That is what unconditional love is all about. It is bound up with forgiveness, tolerance, compassion, acceptance and non-judgement. All of these for ourselves as well as for all others.

Unconditional love! The only kind of love there can ever be! The kind of love Jesus taught us.

Chapter 6

JESUS THE CHRIST

Now it is time to consider the meaning and the connotations of CHRIST.

What do you think Christ means? Who or what do you think Christ is?

Is Christ Jesus Christ?

Is Christ exclusive to Jesus? Does Jesus have a monopoly on Christ?

Contrary to popular belief, the name Christ does not just apply to Jesus. Jesus does not claim a monopoly on that prestigious title! Far from it!

I have a Christ Self. You have a Christ Self. Each and every one of us has a Christ Self. The Christ Self within each of us is our own Higher Self, the point where our human identity and our Spiritual identity meet, our own point of God.

So what is the difference between Jesus, Christ and God?

Jesus was a person, incarnated on this earth 2,000 years ago, in a physical body, and now in the highest echelons of the spiritual hierarchy. God is not a person. God is an energy, the vast total energy of all that is, ever was and ever shall be. Christ is not a person. Christ is not a name. Christ is an energy. Christ is a presence. Christ is a consciousness. And the Christ Energy, the

Christ Consciousness, is the ultimate divine dimension of man, the highest vibrational spiritual level, the very highest level of the Spiritual hierarchy, within the entire God Energy. Christ is the Spiritual potentiality within each one of us, which Jesus too discovered within himself and released. During his incarnation as Yeshua, Jesus of Nazareth 2,000 years ago, Jesus completed his own long struggle to attain '*Christhood*', thereby providing humanity with an example to follow. That was his particular achievement within his lifetime as Jesus, his last incarnation on this earth plane.

There is no Mr, Miss or Mrs Christ!

The term '*Christ'* comes from the Greek word '*Christos',* which means '*anointed'.* Jesus was the man who attained complete '*at-one-ment*' and human-divine unity. And Christ is simply the Greek version of the Hebrew word meaning messiah or savior.

And the Christ Consciousness is that highest degree of Spiritual consciousness that Jesus attained while on this earth. Jesus was called Christ because he became one with his Christ Self and so was anointed with the Light of God, the I AM Presence. But each one of us can equally become one with our own Christ Self. The Christ Consciousness within Jesus is within all of us. We can all attain human-divine unity, the ideal aspiration, a long-term goal, working through many life-times.

Just as Jesus discovered the Higher Self to be the Christ, Gautama discovered it to be the Buddha. Thus, the Higher Self is sometimes called the Inner Christ or Christ Self or the Inner Buddha. Whether we call it the Christ, the Buddha or the Tao, each and every one of us is meant to become one with our own Higher Self.

Jesus came to give us an example of this higher state of consciousness that all of us can achieve. But unfortunately for entire humanity, this has been deliberately kept from people, and ironically, by the very religion that claims to represent Jesus on earth. Instead of portraying Jesus as an example to follow, mainstream Christianity has turned him into an idol to worship, so far removed from us that we will never get to where he is.

When Jesus was alive on earth, and today on the highest vibrational frequency, his desire is to see all of us follow his example and attain the Christ Consciousness, the divine dimension within all of us, so we can do the wonderful deeds he did, and get to where he is.

Right now, at this point in time, there are many people on this earth, in physical embodiment, who actually have the potential to attain full Christ Consciousness or Christhood within this current lifetime. And there are millions more who can attain a high degree of the Christ Consciousness or Christhood within this current lifetime.

"For whosoever will save his life shall lose it; and whosoever will lose his life for my sake shall find it." (Matthew 16:25)

We have already seen what this means.

It means becoming a Christed being, achieving complete Spiritual awareness. It means leaving behind your base, material consciousness and attaining your own Individualised Christ Consciousness.

Mainstream Christian religions tell us that only Jesus can be the Christ because Jesus is God's '*only begotten son'*.

"*And the word was made flesh and dwelt amongst us*." (John 1:14)

But John did not mean by this that Jesus was God's only Son. He simply meant that Jesus, the incarnation of the Word in human flesh, became one with the only Son, which is the Universal Christ Consciousness. But that does not mean that Jesus was the only incarnation of the Universal Christ. And this Universal Christ is individualised for each and every one of us our own Christ Self. As each of us becomes one with our own Christ Self, then we too will be called the Christ, as we become anointed with the Light of the I AM Presence. We are all meant to become the Christ.

Now we can clearly see what Jesus meant by these words:

"But when you pray, go into your room, close the door and pray to your Father, who is unseen." (Matthew 6:6)

Jesus was referring to the secret chamber of your heart when he spoke about going into your room. The mystic Teresa of Avila called this closet her "*interior castle."* Truly entering this closet is going into another dimension of consciousness. Into the dimension of your Higher Self, into the dimension of the Christ Consciousness.

Each and every one of us has the potential to attain individual Christhood, each and every one of us has the potential to be Christed, and attaining our own individual Christhood is the means by which each of us can commune directly with God. We can receive God directly through our own individualised Christ Consciousness, and we do not need to depend on an external, organised church to do that.

God's message was and continues to be delivered to us through those who have attained their Christhood here on earth.

Jesus 2,000 years ago was one such messenger.

The Universal or Collective Christ Consciousness cannot enter this world in its purest form. To enter this world, the Christ Consciousness must be individualised. Individualisation of the Christ Consciousness is not a depleting or degrading process. It is an inclusive process, a liberating process, a process which gives us unlimited potentiality.

"*Flesh and blood cannot enter the kingdom of heaven.*" You cannot experience God through your material consciousness. The problem is that most people have not been taught about individual Christhood, so many sincere and well-meaning people attempt to approach God from the level of their material consciousness.

Christ Consciousness is the mediator between heaven and earth. It is the mediator between the state of consciousness experienced by the Spiritual beings in heaven and the level of consciousness experienced by human beings who are lost in the relativity of the material consciousness.

Look on it as three levels. The bottom, base level is the consciousness of the material world. That's where anger, greed, spite and all negativity hang out. Then there is the Individualised Christ Consciousness, where all is unconditional love, compassion and positivity. Then highest of all is the Collective Christ Consciousness, the Universal Christ Consciousness, which is the

Godhead. The Collective Christ Consciousness cannot descend to earth except through the middle layer, the Individualised Christ Consciousness. Hence the meaning God has no feet but ours, God has no hands but ours, God has no voice but ours.

Similarly we cannot ascend into the Collective Christ Consciousness, the Godhead, except through our own Individualised Christ consciousness.

So, it is obvious! The key to changing the current situation here on planet earth is not the Universal or Collective Christ Consciousness, but the Individualised Christ Consciousness of each and every one of us. Planet earth will only become heaven on earth when more and more of us attain our own individual Christ Consciousness, when more and more of us become Christed beings. Just as Jesus did during his life-time here on planet earth 2,000 years ago.

Chapter 7: Conclusion

YOU ARE GODS!

*"It is written in your own Law that God said 'You are Gods!' " (*John 10:34)

This, as we have seen, was the basis of Jesus' teaching. And:

"The Father and I are one". (John 10:30)

How many times have you tried to justify your actions, how often have you attempted to excuse your behaviour with the words, "*Sure I'm only human!"*

We have all taken refuge behind these words!

Now, having read this book, I hope you realise you are definitely NOT *"only human"!*

Far from it!

The words of Jesus himself confirm that "*You are Gods".* And as such, we have unlimited potentiality.

And we have always been in existence! We have always been in existence and we will always be in existence, as some form or other of energy! As Jesus said:

"*Before Abraham was, I am."* (John 8:58)

We each have duality, we each have two identities. We each have a base, material consciousness and our own higher Christ Consciousness.

What is the difference?

If I hurt someone else intentionally, then I must be in my material base consciousness in order to do that. I cannot possibly do that if I am in my Christ Consciousness. Anger, spite, fear, hatred, revenge all dwell in the lower base material consciousness. So if I am guilty of any of these, then I must be residing in my base material consciousness.

And what about the person whom I have wronged or offended?

The person whom I have just hurt has two choices. He can retaliate and get revenge on me. But if so, than what has he now just done? He has now sunk down, he has now allowed himself to fall down to my level, down into the same base material consciousness as I must be in to allow me to offend him in the first place.

And what is his alternative?

His alternative is to remain steadfastly in his own Christ Consciousness mode or zone and not allow it all to affect him.

From his Christ Consciousness zone, he can see me squirming about down in the gutter, down in the lower base material consciousness and because he is in his Christ Consciousness zone, all he feels for me is pity and compassion for the state into which I have allowed myself to fall.

So it is obvious now what Jesus meant by "*turn the other cheek.*"

(Matthew 5:39) He did not mean literally to turn and let that person give us another blow on the other cheek as well! Ouch! No! Not at all!

Jesus meant turn your other side, your other identity towards that person, your Christ Consciousness zone, and do not descend into the lower base zone of consciousness.

"Father, forgive them, for they know not what they do!" (Luke 23:34)

The ultimate words of forgiveness! Jesus dying on the cross, his body torn and ripped from the knouts that scourged him, his head torn from the thorns pressed into it! And what does he do? He asks for forgiveness for his persecutors. Even making excuses for them! Asking that they be forgiven on account of not knowing what they were doing!

But let us examine these words more closely!

Was Jesus really asking God to forgive them? And why did Jesus need to tell God that they did not know what they were doing? Surely, if that was the case, God would have known that? So what need was there for Jesus to intercede, to beg God for forgiveness for them? It was not God they had just persecuted. It was Jesus.

In reality, what Jesus was doing here was, he was raising himself up into his higher consciousness zone, into his Christ Consciousness zone, identifying with his God essence, that part of him that was divine and immortal, and as he was now in that zone, there was no anger, no desire for revenge, no desire for retaliation of any kind. Just pity and compassion for them, squirming about down there in their base consciousness, in the mud and gutter, because that was where they must have been in order to do what they did!

So, the message is clear!

We need to raise ourselves up out of the base material earth consciousness, where we hate, we kill, we insult, we hurt and we get involved in all the other base, foul deeds and thoughts that reside in that zone, and in that zone only.

We need to raise our consciousness up into our own lighter, higher Individualised Christ Consciousness zone, where we see with pity and compassion those down below us squirming about, stuck in the mire and the dross, unable to extricate themselves and move up higher. When we see everything from such a vantage point, there is no need for forgiveness, for forgiveness is intrinsically and inherently bound up with our pity and compassion.

And it was from his Christ Consciousness zone, and not from any human base zone, that Jesus was able to perform his so-called 'miracles' and healings.

And indeed, it is from the Christ Consciousness zone, that higher, purer, lighter zone within each of us, that modern day holistic therapists, Reiki practitioners and Spiritual healers and teachers work. It is simply just not possible to do such work from the base, material consciousness level.

And to be able to do what Jesus did, to be the Gods he told us we all are, to fulfil our unlimited potentiality, then we must be in our own Individualised Christ Consciousness zone.

And when we arrive at that point of meeting with God within our own selves, then we see the wonders the universe has to offer us.

It is then we live in the present, knowing that everything we need and want is already out there, just waiting for us to draw it towards ourselves.

It is then we see that the kingdom of heaven truly lies within each one of us.

It is then we realise that we are living the teachings of Jesus as he meant us to live them.

So now let me explain the front cover of this book and why I chose that particular illustration.

There are three vertical bodies in that picture. The bottom body is the material body, the physical embodiment of each one of us on planet earth at this point in time. In other words, that lower body is you in your base consciousness, your material consciousness state, sometimes called the death consciousness. When you are in that state, you are immersed in the things of this world. You are immersed in material possessions and getting more and more. This is the land of the self. This is the land of the human ego. When you are dwelling in this zone, you are expressing anger, resentment, jealousy, desire for revenge, pride, unwillingness to forgive and all the other negative attributes that dwell in this base zone. All these negative feelings and emotions are simply states of consciousness. If you are given to expressing any of these, then you must be in your base zone, your base consciousness, because it is only from your base consciousness zone that you can project any of this negativity.

Now look at the middle body of the three.

This is you in your Individualised Christ Consciousness. This is you as a Christed being. This is you when you have raised your consciousness above the base material level of consciousness. You are no longer the same dense matter as you were in your base material consciousness. Your vibration has been raised, you are now vibrating at a faster rate, simply because your energy is lighter, higher and brighter. And why? Because you are now dwelling in your Individualised Christ zone.

See the difference?

In this Individualised Christ zone you are still the unique you, but you now are observing what is going on in the base zone below you, rather than being involved in it as you were when you were dwelling in that base material zone. Now you do not retaliate, you do not entertain thoughts of revenge, anger, resentment, or any of the other attributes that we saw reside in the lower consciousness level. And why not? Simply because those negative attributes do not reside in this Christ Consciousness zone. You are operating from pure unconditional love and light. And of course, forgiveness. When someone insults or hurts you intentionally, then instead of reacting, which is exactly what they want you to do, you immediately recognise that that person must be in his base material zone in order to do that. And so you feel pity for that individual down there in the gutter, that individual squirming about down there in that lower level of consciousness, trying to pull others down to his own level.

And in just the same way as you do not kick a dog when it is down, neither do you kick anyone who is down in the gutter. Instead, you look down on them from your higher vantage point and you feel compassion and pity for them. You see them as the bright Spiritual beings they really are, underneath all the negativity and evil which is masking that bright Spiritual light.

This was how Jesus could forgive his persecutors. He had managed to raise himself into his Individualised Christ Consciousness zone. He was a Christed being. He had achieved what he came here to achieve for himself!

Now look at the highest of the three bodies.

This is the Collective Christ Consciousness, the highest energy level within the totality that is God. This is where we are all heading, this is where we will all end up. Jesus has just got there before us, and that is how he is able to show us the way, to show us how we too can attain our Individualised Christ Consciousness, just like he has done. There are millions and trillions of souls already at that level, and millions of more souls now very near.

Look again at the picture. Now consider this.

The highest being is the Collective Christ Consciousness. Now see how this Collective Christ Consciousness, God, cannot descend directly to the earth plane? The only way in which God, the Christ Consciousness energy, can descend into this earth plane dense energy level is through each one of us, through our Individualised

Christ Consciousness.

Yes! God has no voice but ours! God has no hands but ours! God has no feet but ours! God works through us in our Individualised Christ Consciousness state!

Now consider this! If God cannot descend directly down to the earth plane, but only by descending down through our Individualised Christ Consciousness state, then it is obvious that we cannot access the Collective Christ Consciousness zone directly from our base material consciousness zone! We must ascend first through our own Individualised Christ Consciousness zone before we gain access to the highest zone.

It all makes so much sense!

And when we arrive at the pearly gates, as we saw in an earlier chapter, our soul will gravitate automatically to a particular level of vibrational energy within the intricate hierarchy of energy levels that permeate the celestial kingdoms. And what exactly will determine what level your soul gravitates towards?

The differentiating criteria for each newly arriving soul is not how many good deeds you did while here on earth or how much money you gave to charity, or even how often or how fervently you prayed. No, not at all!

The one criteria, the one deciding factor that determines where your soul goes is, what consciousness level are you on?

There you have it!

It's all about consciousness levels and moving up from your base material consciousness level where you are engaged in negativity, and attaining your Individualised Christ Consciousness level, the intermediary stage between you and the Collective Christ Consciousness, God. And when you dwell in this, your Individualised Christ Consciousness level, then you are living your life as you are meant to live it.

Then you are exemplifying the words that Jesus spoke to us!

"ARE YE NOT GODS, AS I AM?"

"WHAT I DO, YOU ALSO CAN DO, AND MORE!"

This is us in our Individualised Christ Consciousness!

Happy days!

I leave the last words to Jesus:

"You are like salt for the whole human race. But if salt loses its saltiness, there is no way to make it salty again. It has become worthless, so it is thrown out and people trample on it.

You are like light for the whole world. A city built on a hill cannot be hidden. No one lights a lamp and puts it under a bowl; instead he puts it on the lampstand, where it gives light for everyone in the house. In the same way your light must shine before people." (Matthew 5:13)

So, from your own Individualised Christ Consciousness zone, let your beautiful light shine forth, spreading warmth, comfort, love and joy to all around you!

Until we meet again!

Namaste!

Made in the USA
Columbia, SC
12 April 2017